B.R. 827

A SEAMAN'S POCKET-BOOK

June 1943

By Authority of the
LORDS COMMISSIONERS OF THE ADMIRALTY

Introduced by Brian Lavery

LONDON

CONWAY
BLOOMSBURY
LONDON • NEW DELHI • NEW YORK • SYDNEY

INTRODUCTION

When John Davies entered the Royal Navy as an Ordinary Seaman in 1941, his petty officer told him, "You can't learn nothin' from a bleedin' book." Fortunately the Admiralty did not share that attitude. Through its various branches it produced numerous textbooks, some clear and readable, some technical and opaque.

The idea of a seaman's manual originated more than three centuries earlier, with John Smith's *Sea Grammar* of 1627. That, and works such as D'Arcy Lever's *Young Sea Officer's Sheet Anchor* of 1808, were aimed at midshipmen rather than ordinary seamen, who were rarely literate and could not afford to buy books.

In the 1850s the Admiralty began to train its own seamen rather then recruiting them from the merchant service. To cater for this, C Burney produced *A Boy's Manual of Seamanship and Gunnery* in 1869, and later editions were published by the Admiralty. In 1908–9 the Admiralty produced its own *Manual of Seamanship* in two volumes – the first for boys in the training establishments and for the early training of cadets, the second for the further training of officers and petty officers. It acknowledged its debt to several other publications and had grown by accretion; there was no introduction, little attempt to organise material systematically, to write clearly and simply, or edit out material which the ordinary rating was unlikely to understand. A revised and slightly simplified edition was produced in 1932-37, still in two volumes.

This is where matters stood in 1943. Volume I was issued to every entrant to the seaman branch and was reprinted many times as the navy expanded from 73,000 men at the outbreak of war to 660,000 in the middle of 1943. Captain H P K Oram came to the Admiralty from the cruiser *Hawkins* and cast a critical and experienced eye over training methods. The navy was preparing for its biggest ever expansion for the Normandy invasion, and it would take on more than 100,000 men over the next year. Volume I of the *Manual of Seamanship* was due to reprint, but it was more than 450 pages long and paper was in short supply. Furthermore,

It has been found that the Seamanship Manual, Volume I, contains too much detail and too much advanced seamanship for training of the hostilities-only seamen, with the result that the majority are unable to absorb the essential elementary knowledge required.

[ADM 1/16601]

In April 1943 Oram called a meeting of the training commanders of the schools for wartime ordinary seamen, or 'hostilities only' men. It was agreed to produce a new and much shorter manual, which would continue to serve a dual purpose. It would give new seamen 'a Pocket Book containing the seamanlike knowledge required of them during training and their first six months at sea.' It would also serve as a primer for officer candidates, who had to serve some time as junior ratings before beginning officer training. A hundred thousand were needed for new entries, plus 11,500 for other purposes.

The drawings were produced by the instructional staff of the seamen's training establishment *King Alfred*, largely in their spare time, and Lieutenant-Commander Crick was commended for writing it. The first draft was ready by the middle of May but after that the project slowed down as it passed through various Admiralty departments, and paper supply was difficult. It was August before the galley proofs were sent, and late November before the first copies were delivered.

The book was given the number BR 827, meaning Book of Reference rather than a confidential book, which should be kept secret. The *Seaman's Pocket-Book* was on sale to the public at a price of 1s 3d or approximately 6p, though of course the great majority of copies were issued free to seamen.

The book is specific in its aims. It says little to stokers, writers or stewards who had their own handbooks. It is very definitely a manual of seamanship, with little of the material on naval organisation which filled much of its predecessors. It says nothing about the skills which most seamen would learn after their basic training, for these were in manuals on gunnery, torpedo, anti-submarine and eventually radar.

The *Seaman's Pocket-Book* has a friendly introduction to explain its aims, and its drawings, for example Fig 15 on the tides and Fig 17 on steering a ship, are far clearer than before. Unlike some other Admiralty publications it truly was a pocket book, even in the restricted space in the seaman's 'square rig' uniform. It covered many aspects of seamanship in a clear and concise manner. The chapter on 'The Sea' was largely new. The final chapter, on 'Ship Safety', was completely new, for the navy had paid little attention to such matters until a series of disasters such as the loss of the *Ark Royal* in 1941. That part was also relevant to non-seamen, and was printed separately as BR 827A

The *Pocket-Book* was issued by Admiralty Fleet Order of December 1943. It was in time to train many of the seamen who entered in the following year, forming a large part of the crews of landing craft and support ships for the invasion of Normandy. Flag signals are rarely used today and the system of buoyage has changed, but most chapters – on the sea and its tides or on ropework, for example – are as relevant today as they ever were.

Brian Lavery is the author of *Churchill's Navy: The Ships, Men & Organisation 1939–1945* (Conway, 2006)

SEA SENSE

His Majesty's ships or vessels, from the battleship to the smallest unit, are specially designed to do their particular duty. The **Fleet** operates **as a team**, each member playing its part.

During peace or war there are hazards of wind and sea, fog and shoal, fire and collision, which may be a source of menace to every vessel from the moment she is launched. Generations of seamen dealing successfully with these dangers have handed down their experience to the seamen of to-day. **Seamanship** is the art of ship management and maintenance, and the capacity to use foresight and common sense, to make fullest use of seamen's experience.

No warship has room for 'passengers' who stand about indifferent to what is going on around them. The seaman must develop **sea sense**, just as the driver of a motor vehicle develops 'road sense.' He must be alert continually to visualize what is happening, and to anticipate what might happen next. A true seaman is always ready to act in time to avoid injury to his ship or to his shipmates, or to himself. He does the right thing because he has learned how the sea behaves, and how it affects a ship afloat, and how she can be kept under control in spite of it.

There is no mystery about it, although many unfamiliar terms are used. These are necessary because things happen too quickly at sea to allow time for long and detailed instructions. Orders must be short and snappy, and they must be instantly and exactly obeyed.

So there are terms which distinguish clearly the different parts of a ship from one another, the relative positions of objects in or outside the ship, and the direction in which they lie. There are expressions describing the movement of objects on board, and the movement of the ship herself.

When a man chosen to play football for a team is allotted his place on the field he must learn a number of football terms and expressions before he can be of any use to his side. In the same way, every man called to serve afloat must recognise his responsibility to his shipmates. He must lose no time in acquiring **sea sense**, so that he can play his part in the team.

CONTENTS

CHAPTER I

SEA TERMS

THE PARTS OF A SHIP
Ends and Sides

The main body of a ship is called the **hull**.

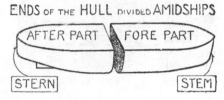

ENDS of the HULL divided AMIDSHIPS

FIG. 1

There are two ways of dividing the hull into two equal parts, just as there are two ways of splitting a sausage. You can cut it across the middle, from side to side, as in Fig. 1, dividing the **fore part** from the **after part**. The extreme end of the fore part is called the **stem**. The extreme end of the after part is called the **stern**. The two parts meet amidships.

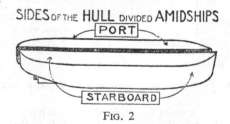

SIDES of the HULL divided AMIDSHIPS

FIG. 2

Or you can cut the hull down the middle from end to end, along what is called the **fore-and-aft midship line**, dividing the two sides. Looking towards the stem, the left-hand half will be the **port** half of the hull, and the right-hand half will be the **starboard** half.

In both cases the line of division runs **amidships**—*i.e.*, in the middle of the ship.

7

Surfaces

The **hull** has a **port side** and a **starboard side**. These sides meet underneath in the keel, in the fore part at the stem, and in the after part at the stern.

When the ship is afloat the sides above the **waterline** round the hull are called the **ship's side**, and the sides below the waterline are called the **bottom**.

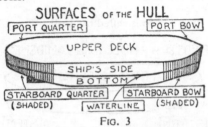

SURFACES OF THE HULL

Fig. 3

The hull surfaces in the fore part, which are rounded to meet the stem, are called the **bows** (port bow and starboard bow).

The corresponding surfaces of the after part are called the **quarters** (port and starboard quarters).

Horizontal surfaces in a ship are called **decks**; those which are exposed to the weather are called the **upper deck**.

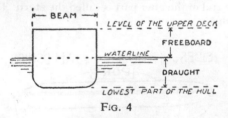

Fig. 4

The height of a ship's upper deck above the waterline is her **freeboard**.

The height of the waterline above the lowest part of the ship (keel, or propellers if below the keel) is called her **draught**. She is said to 'draw' so many feet of water.

Names are given to parts of the upper deck, and to decks on lower levels. The after end of the upper deck between the quarters is the **quarterdeck**. The fore end of the upper deck between the bows is the **forecastle** (foc'sle). The remaining deck between them is called the **waist**.

DECKS

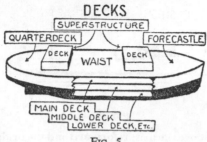

Fig. 5

Any part of the hull which is built above the upper deck is called a **superstructure**, having its own **deck** on top, its port and starboard sides, its fore side, and its after side. The decks below are called the **main deck, middle deck, lower deck, platform decks, etc.,** according to the size of the ship.

TERMS DESCRIBING DIRECTION

From any point in the ship, towards the **bows** is **forward** (for'ard), towards the stern is **aft**. Across the ship from side to side is **athwartships.**

TERMS DESCRIBING POSITION

The seaman speaks of serving in a certain ship. When he joins her he goes **on board**. The ladder by which he ascends the ship's side is said to be rigged **outboard** (*i.e.,* projecting beyond and outside the hull). When he steps **inboard** (*i.e.,* inside the rails round the ship's side) he finds himself **on deck**. He is given a berth in a mess **between decks** (inside the ship), and to reach it he goes **below**. A landsman would say 'indoors' and 'downstairs.' In a ship a **ladder** gives access to the deck above, through a **hatch**, a square opening in the deck.

On shore one may speak of the 'right' and 'left' sides or the 'north side' and 'south side' of a building, but as this is not possible in a ship the positions of objects on board are reckoned in two directions, viz.:

(1) **Fore and aft**—*i.e.,* relative to the *ends* of the ship.
(2) **Athwartships**—*i.e.,* across the ship, relative to the *sides* of the ship.

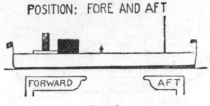

FIG. 6

In the sketch above the mast is **forward** and the bridge and funnel are **aft**. **Right aft** is an ensign staff, and **right forward** is a jack staff. A man is standing **amidships**.

Comparing positions of objects with one another, the funnel is **abaft** the bridge, the bridge is **abaft** the mast, but **forward of** the funnel.

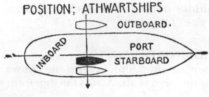

FIG. 7

Reckoning athwartships, objects actually on the fore-and-aft line are said to be amidships. Elsewhere they are described as lying to port or starboard.

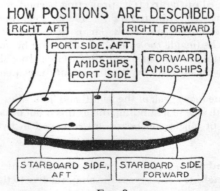

FIG. 8

In Fig. 7, opposite, a ship is carrying three boats, one of which is swung **outboard** to port.

Inboard she carries two boats to starboard. Comparing the relative positions of the two boats when both lie inboard on the same side of the deck, the black boat lies **inboard** of the white boat, and the white boat is said to lie outboard of the black boat.

The position of an object can be clearly described by combining the two methods of reckoning, as in Fig. 8.

GENERAL TERMS

The width of a ship measured athwartships is her **beam**. The beam of a ship, when speaking of overall dimensions, means the width at the widest point of the hull.

Ships are divided into compartments by walls termed **bulkheads**. Access to these compartments is by doors or hatches, designed, when closed, to keep the compartment watertight.

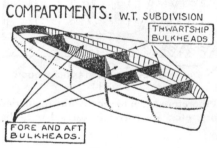

COMPARTMENTS: W.T. SUBDIVISION

THWARTSHIP BULKHEADS

FORE AND AFT BULKHEADS.

Fig. 9

The household terms 'ceiling' and 'floor' are to be avoided, as naturally they are 'decks' in a ship. Underfoot is 'the deck,' and overhead is the 'deck-head,' and its supporting 'beams.' Some decks are given additional support by pillars known as **stanchions**.

Light is admitted through **ports** cut in the ship's side, made watertight by hinged **scuttles** of thick glass, secured by wing-nuts, and reinforced by **deadlights** for darkening ship, and to keep the compartment watertight if the scuttle glass should be broken.

If the decks were open from end to end damage to the hull at any point which allowed water to enter would cause the ship to fill up and sink. Watertight (W.T.) bulkheads limit flooding to the compartments nearest the damage, provided that all openings such as doors, scuttles, and hatches, can be made watertight and are closed in time. As these openings cannot be closed against an inrush of water, as many as possible are kept permanently closed at sea, while others are only opened by permission of the Officer of the Watch (O.O.W.).

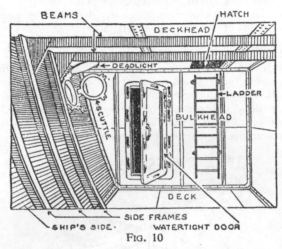

Fig. 10

Great care is therefore taken to see that the regulations concerning watertight doors, etc., are correctly carried out, that Watertight (W.T.)

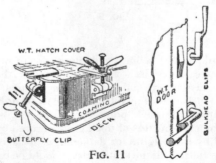

Fig. 11

fittings are properly closed, and that every seaman appreciates what steps are necessary to render any compartment watertight.

POSITIONS OF OUTSIDE OBJECTS RELATIVE TO THE SHIP

Alongside: side by side, and touching.
Abreast: level with, in line with.
Abeam: directly at right angles to the fore-and-aft line.
Ahead: directly in advance.
Astern: directly in rear.

Abeam, ahead, and **astern** are **bearings**—that is, they point to definite directions. In addition, when an object is bearing on the **bow**

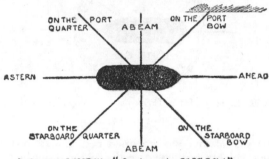

I. GENERAL DIRECTION: "Smoke on the PORT BOW"

FIG. 12

it is midway between ahead and abeam; when it bears **on the quarter** it is midway between abeam and astern. These terms are often used to indicate the general direction of an object.

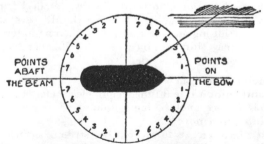

II More definitely, to the nearest POINT. (A point = 11¼°)
"Object bearing 3 POINTS on the PORT BOW."

FIG. 13

Rather more accurately, the bearing may be estimated in points on the bow or in points abaft the beam (a 'point' is 11¼°, or ⅛ of a right angle).

Still more precisely, the bearings of objects (*e.g.*, reports by lookouts) are given to the nearest degree from right ahead through 180° to right astern.

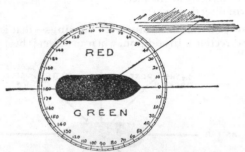

Ⅲ. Exactly: "RED Three Four, a Ship !"

Fig. 14

The port side of the ship is named **red**; the starboard side is **green**. These colours are the same as the coloured side lights that are carried for navigational safety. Thus, **"Red 90"** means "exactly abeam to port"; **"Green 45"** means "on the starboard **bow**"; **"Red 135"** means "on the port quarter," or "4 points abaft the beam"; and so on.

MOVEMENTS OF OBJECTS ON BOARD

A seaman speaks of going 'forward,' 'below,' 'on deck,' and 'aloft' (*i.e.*, anywhere in the rigging of a mast). He uses the same expressions for shifting an object, always reckoning in terms of the ship; thus, he may shift an object 'aft,' or 'further forward,' or 'inboard' or 'nearer the ship's side.'

To **launch** is to drag an object along.

To **lift and launch** is to lift the weight clear before each heave.

To **ship** is to place an object in position.

To **unship** is to remove it.

To **fend** a boat, etc., is to prevent her striking against anything that might endanger her; hence, boat's fender.

To **fleet** is to shift the position of.

MOVEMENT OF THE SHIP

A vessel is **under way** when she is not at anchor, or made fast to a buoy or to the shore, or aground.

When actually moving through the water she has **way** on her; if moving too fast she is said to have 'too much way on.' When she is moving bows first she is moving ahead, making **headway**; if stern first she is moving **astern**, making **sternway**. She is said to **gather way** when she begins to move through the water. She has **steerage way** when she is moving with sufficient way to be steered. A vessel moving sideways is said to be moving **broadside** to port or starboard; if she is under way, and is being blown sideways by the wind, she is said to be making leeway.

The **ship's head** is the direction in which her bows are pointing at a given moment.

The **course** is the direction, by compass, in which the ship is travelling.

The **wake** is that part of the track immediately astern of her.

The **heel** of a ship is the angle between her masts and the vertical to the earth's surface, when she inclines to one side. She is said to have a **list** if she heels permanently to one side.

The **trim** of a ship describes the condition in which she floats in the water; *e.g.,* she may 'list to port,' or trim 'by the head' (*i.e.,* deeper in the water forward than aft) or 'by the stern' (the opposite).

The normal **trim** of a ship depends on the **buoyancy**, or ability to float, of her ends and her sides, and she may be **trimmed** by adjusting the position of weights in her hull until she floats level.

Ballast is any additional weight at a particular point which is required to trim ship.

Aweigh: when the anchor is broken out of the ground.

Adrift: broken from moorings; driven at random by wind and tide.

Afloat or **waterborne:** floating on the surface.

Waterlogged: full of water, but still floating.

Awash: level with the surface of the water.

Riding: A vessel 'rides' to her anchor or to a buoy when properly secured.

Tide-rode: The position of a vessel at anchor when, owing to the wind and tide setting in different directions, the vessel takes up a position heading between the two.

Weather side: the side of the ship that faces the wind.

Lee side: the sheltered side of the ship. Those who are subject to sea-sickness will be unpopular if they do not use this side.

CHAPTER II
THE SEA

THE **depth of the sea** ('soundings') is measured in fathoms, a fathom being equal to six feet.

Distance at sea is measured in *nautical miles*. A nautical or sea mils is 6,080 feet. A *cable*, as a measure used by seamen, is 200 yards, or 100 fathoms, and is approximately one-tenth of a nautical mile.

Speed at sea is measured in nautical miles per hour, called **knots**. A *knot* is a speed, and should never be used to express a distance.

If a ship is going at a rate of 30 nautical miles per hour she is said to be going '30 knots.' (As the nautical mile is longer than the land mile this represents a land speed of 34½ m.p.h.)

The Effect of Wind on the Sea Surface

When one part of the earth's surface is warmer than the part next to it, air flows from the cooler part to take the place of air rising from the warmer part. This is because warm air rises, and causes a drop in pressure at the warm spot, which adjacent higher pressures hasten to fill up, or equalize.

The movement of air at any point is the **wind**.

The **barometer** measures atmospheric pressure, and helps the seaman, watching the rate of rise and fall of pressure, to forecast the wind's direction and force. He can thus anticipate any change in the weather.

A wind is named by the direction it is blowing **from**; thus, a 'north' wind blows from north towards south.

Wind is said to **veer** if it shifts in the direction of the hands of a clock, and to **back** if it shifts in the opposite direction. Thus, a north wind veering will go round eastwards; an east wind backing will go round towards the north, and so on.

The force of the wind is estimated from the Beaufort scale given at the beginning of the ship's logbook. In the logbook every ship records the day's events, courses steered, work done, etc., and details of the weather and state of the sea and visibility.

Visibility is expressed as the furthest distance at which a seaman can distinguish an object. The distance depends on the height of eye above sea level, the clarity of the atmosphere, and the way the light strikes the object.

With increasing force of wind the surface of the sea becomes disturbed and **waves** are formed. A wave travels along the surface of the sea before the wind, the water itself merely rising and falling as the wave passes. (When a rope laid out along the deck is given a smart jerk upwards at one end, the wave travels the whole length of the rope; note that it is the wave that moves forward—not the rope).

The highest part of a wave is the crest, and the lowest part between two successive waves is the **trough**. A wave is steepest on its advancing side. When the force of the wind is such that the crest falls forward the wave is said to **break**. A sea breaking on board is likely to sweep away anything not securely lashed down.

When a wind has been blowing from the same quarter for some time a **swell** is produced. This is a wave formation on a very much larger scale, but the distance apart of tops of successive swells is greater in proportion to their height, giving the effect of large areas of sea rising and falling slowly, with waves travelling across their surface if the wind is still blowing.

Note that a wave is caused by the actual wind at a place, whereas a **swell** is caused by recent wind, or wind at a distance.

Effect of a Sea on a Ship

A ship steaming with her bows meeting the seas end on is said to be meeting a 'head sea.' Steaming with her stern to wind she is said to be running before a 'following sea.' In either case her bows and stern will alternately rise and fall in a **pitching** movement. With the wind abeam she has a 'beam sea,' and is made to **roll,** heeling alternately from side to side.

The 'stiffness' of a ship indicates her readiness to recover normal trim when forced out of it by wind or sea. She rights herself by using the weights disposed in her hull in leverage with the buoyancy of her hull.

Hove to: deliberately remaining stationary, or very nearly stationary, to avoid damage to the ship.

Broach to: falling into the trough of a sea, more or less broadside on. When running with the wind on the quarter, bad steering or a sea striking the stern may cause a ship to broach to. This is dangerous.

Green sea: A vessel is said to be 'shipping it green' when solid masses of water are coming on board in a heavy sea. A green sea will sweep away anything not properly secured.

TIDES

When a ship is lying alongside a jetty it will be noticed that she rises and falls with the tide. Generally speaking, it will be found that after a tide has reached its lowest level, **at low water**, it then rises for about 6¼ hours until it reaches its highest level at **high water**, after which it falls during another 6¼ hours to the next **low water**, and so on.

There are two high waters and two low waters every twenty-five hours, **high water** occurring about *fifty minutes later each day*.

The heights and times of successive tides, which vary from day to day, are to be found in the **Tide Tables**, a publication in which the time and height of tides is predicted for every day of the year at a number of different ports.

It will be found that the rise and fall of tide is most marked about the time of new moon and full moon (**spring tides**), and least marked 7½ days later in each case (**neap tides**).

A vessel grounding on a falling tide, say one hour after high water, will not float again until one hour before the next high water, a matter of ten hours.

A vessel grounding at high water, say two days after springs, need not expect to float without assistance until two days before the next springs, a matter of ten days.

When under way the seaman is careful to avoid these misfortunes by taking frequent **soundings** to satisfy himself that his vessel has plenty of water to float. When alongside he tends his shore lines to suit the rise and fall of the tide.

TIDAL STREAMS

The vertical movement of water at a place, such as a jetty in harbour, is the result of the **tidal wave**. The tidal wave also produces horizontal movements, in and out of harbours and along the coast, called tidal streams.

A rising tide is accompanied by the **flood** stream. A falling tide is accompanied by the **ebb** stream.

In the course of time the ebb and flow of these tidal streams may carve out channels in the sea-bed, throwing up banks and shoals between them. The water in such channels is known as the **tideway**, and may be expected to ebb seawards for about six hours, then slack, then turn and flow for six hours in the opposite direction, until it becomes slack water again at high water.

Indication of the *set*, or direction, of the stream is given by ships riding head to tide, buoys slanting away from it, objects drifting with it, posts standing in it with water rippling in their wake, etc. By reading

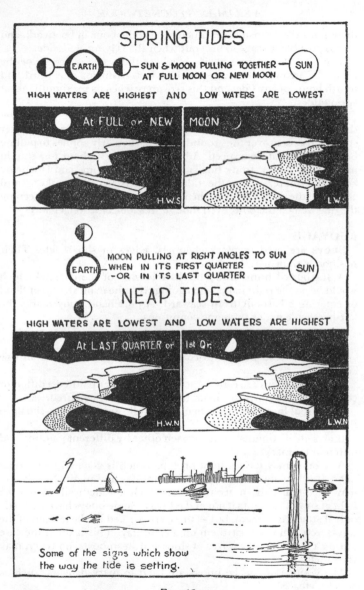

FIG. 15

these signs the seaman saves much time and labour in boatwork, and avoids possible damage to his craft when she is lying alongside.

The tidal stream runs stronger where the water is deeper or the channel narrower. The stream runs fastest during the third and fourth hours of any tide, and this stream reaches its maximum rate at spring tides.

It is important to realise that the speed and course of a vessel through the water may differ considerably in a tideway from her speed and course over the ground. This particularly applies to pulling boats and craft at slow speed. A boat pulling up harbour to a ship in midstream, with a strong tide against her, saves time and labour by keeping inshore, where the tidal stream is usually weaker, until abreast of the mark aimed at, then making across to the mark, keeping the tide well on the bow, even though this looks the longer way.

BUOYAGE

Buoys are used to mark channels, edges of shoals, etc. Their position is shown on the charts.

A **starboard hand buoy** marks that side of the channel which would be on the right hand when going with the main stream of flood or entering a harbour from seaward. A port hand buoy marks the left-hand side under the same conditions.

IN THE UNITED KINGDOM

Starboard hand buoys are conical in shape and painted all one colour.

Port hand buoys are can-shaped, and are either painted a different colour from the starboard hand buoys or are particoloured.

Spherical buoys are used to mark middle grounds—*i.e.*, shoals in the middle of a channel.

Buoys are distinguished from each other by different painting and different topmarks.

Any buoy may have a light on top, which is generally a flashing light. It is usually lit by gas and is alight day and night. New buoys may be fitted with an arrangement which automatically lights the light at sunset and puts it out at daybreak. Some buoys have a whistle or bell attached to them, but as these are worked by the motion of the waves you will not hear them on a calm day. This is often the case during a fog. The bow waves of ships and steamboats, however, may start them off.

Many kinds of special buoys are used to mark dangers, such as wrecks, etc.

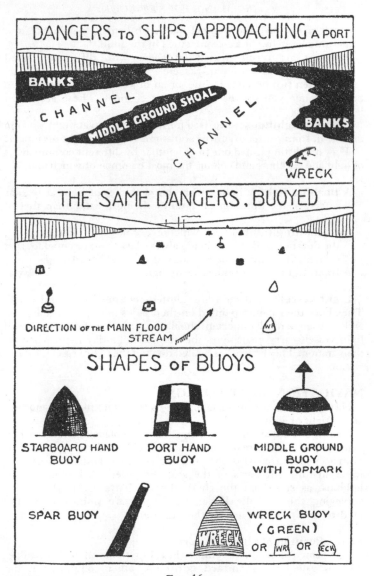

Fig. 16

Small rivers have the channel marked by small spar buoys, and sometimes branches of a tree are stuck in the mud.

Beacons are posts erected on shore with different shaped topmarks for use as leading marks, etc.

Very often two beacons in line, or an object ashore in line with a beacon, guide you up the middle of a channel. These are called leading marks.

Lights or **lighthouses** are used for fixing the ship at night, and are usually lit from sunset to sunrise, but some are kept alight for longer.

They are distinguished one from another by different combinations of light and darkness and colour, the most common of which are:

A flashing light: a light which shows flashes of light at regular intervals, the duration of darkness being greater than that of light.

An occulting light: a light which every now and then goes out, the duration of darkness being always less than, or equal to, that of light. If a light changes colour, it is called alternating.

A fixed light: a continuous steady light.

Light vessels in Britain are painted red and in Ireland black. They have their names painted on their sides in large white letters, and are used to mark important shoals for purposes of navigation. All light vessels carry a shape on the mast called a day mark when on their station. The daymark is hauled down if the light vessel is off her station.

NAVIGATION AND PILOTAGE

Navigation is the art of taking ships from one place to another, out of sight of land.

Pilotage is the art of taking ships from one place to another when land or navigational marks are in sight. This is done by the aid of **charts**, which are maps showing the coastline and the depths of water in different parts of the sea, the latter marked in feet or fathoms, as stated on the chart. These charts are made by the surveying ships of the Royal Navy, and are published by the Hydrographic Department of the Admiralty.

Fixing Position of Ship on Chart

The principal magnetic compass in a ship stands on the forebridge. This is called the **standard compass**, other compasses at the different steering positions being called 'steering compasses.' In ships fitted with gyro compasses (see page 29) the 'repeaters' take the place of steering compasses, or are placed alongside them.

The standard compass is housed in a **binnacle**, or wooden stand, placed where a good all-round view can be obtained, which raises the compass card above the level of surrounding bridge screens, etc. When the brass hood covering the binnacle is removed it will be seen that an instrument called an **azimuth mirror** is fitted on top of the compass bowl, and that this instrument can be trained round in any direction. When the officer conning the ship wishes to obtain the direction, called the **bearing**, of any object from the compass card he trains the azimuth mirror round until he can see both the object over the top of the mirror and the reflection of the compass card in the mirror. He is then able to read off the compass bearing.

When within sight of land the position of the ship is obtained by taking bearings by compass of two or more prominent objects marked on the chart. These bearings are then drawn on the chart in pencil. The point where the lines cut is the position of the ship.

When out of sight of land the position of the ship is obtained by observations of heavenly bodies with a sextant. This is only possible when the horizon is clear. These observations are called **sights**. If no observations are obtained the position of the ship must be found by calculation from the course and the speed since the last fix was obtained. This is called 'dead reckoning.'

The courses steered by the standard compass are drawn in pencil on the chart.

The **speed through the water** is found from patent logs and the revolutions of the engines.

The amount the ship has been drifted, owing to currents, tidal streams, and wind, must be allowed for to obtain the course and speed made good **over the ground**. Hence the need for careful steering and accurate working of logs.

Speed through the Water

(1) **Revolutions.** A table of speeds at various revolutions per minute of the engines is prepared by steaming the ship at these revolutions over a measured mile and noting the elapsed times.

(2) **Patent Logs.** In the **'towed type'** a rotor is streamed astern at a convenient distance. Its blades cause it to revolve a certain number of times every mile, like a speedometer. It is connected to a dial which enables these revolutions to be read off as distance run. Speed is found by noting elapsed time.

The '*pitometer*' type consists of an open tube beneath the hull, in which water pressure builds up as speed increases. It is capable of recording very high speeds. Dials indicate speed through the water and distance run.

The *'Chernikeef'* type consists of a miniature propeller exposed beneath the hull. When caused to revolve as the ship drags it through the water it measures distance run. It is capable of recording at very low speeds. Dials indicate speed through the water and distance run.

Depth of Water

In the sea-bed are hills and valleys (shoals and channels), hidden beneath the surface of the sea. Where there is not enough water over the top of a shoal a ship must feel her way round it, keeping to the channel. Hence the need for accurate soundings.

Soundings are measured by the following methods:

(1) **Echo-sounding Gear.** A transmitter in the bottom of the ship emits a sound impulse which travels outward through the sea at uniform speed. On reaching the ocean bed part of the sound is reflected and returns to the ship in the form of an echo, where its arrival is picked up by hydrophone.

The hydrophone passes the echo on to a receiver, which measures the interval of time between impulse and echo; and as the velocity of sound in water is known, the receiver converts the elapsed time into soundings by mechanism which provides a continuous record of depths on a strip of paper.

(2) **Kelvin Sounding Machine.** Casts of the deep sea lead may be taken at intervals with this machine, and soundings obtained by two methods:

(*a*) The depth may be read off on a boxwood scale by noting the penetration of sea water up a chemically coated glass tube, sealed at the upper end, which has been lowered to the sea-bed in a case attached to the lead. The pressure of water effecting penetration increases with the depth.

(*b*) Having noted the exact length of wire run out until the lead reaches the bottom, the depth may be calculated by reference to a speed-depth table. Obviously the amount of wire run out increases both with the speed of ship and with the depth of water; accuracy is therefore dependent on uniform braking of the reel of wire. The bottom of the lead is hollowed out and may be filled with tallow, which is called 'arming'; the nature of the bottom will be shown by the sand, stones, etc., which are sticking to the arming. The nature of the bottom is frequently as much value in finding the position of the ship as is depth of water.

(3) Hand lead and line, subject to certain limitations of speed, depth, and the height of the leadsman above the waterline.

USE OF THE HAND LEAD AND LINE

The weight of the hand lead is from 10 to 14 lb. It is bar-shaped, and is fitted at the top with a hide becket. The hand lead can be armed in the same way as the deep sea lead.

The line is of 1⅛ inch, and is 25 fathoms in length; it is bent to the lead by running a long eye splice, made at the end of the line, through the hide becket on the head of the lead, and then passing the lead through the eye.

The lead line is marked as follows:

At	2 fathoms	. .	Two strips of leather.
,,	3 ,,	. .	Three ,, ,, ,,
,,	5 ,,	. .	A piece of white bunting.
,,	7 ,,	. .	,, ,, ,, red ,,
,,	10 ,,	. .	,, ,, ,, leather with a hole in it.
,,	13 ,,	. .	,, ,, ,, blue bunting.
,,	15 ,,	. .	,, ,, ,, white ,,
,,	17 ,,	. .	,, ,, ,, red ,,
,,	20 ,,	. .	Two knots.

Aids to Memory

The marks are:

White = 5 letters = five and fifteen fathoms.
Red = **crimson** = 7 letters = seven and seventeen fathoms.
Blue = 4 letters = 1 and 3 = thirteen fathoms.

The hole in the leather at ten fathoms represents the nought in 10.

When using a longer line than 25 fathoms the line is marked with 1 knot at each 5 fathoms, and with 3, 4, 5, etc., knots at 30, 40, 50, etc., fathoms respectively.

The fathoms at 1, 4, 6, 8, 9, 11, 12, 14, 16, 18, 19 are not marked, and are called 'deeps.'

To Heave the Lead

Ships are generally fitted with a platform on each side of the forecastle, which is called the **chains**.

If no platform is fitted the lead can be hove from the sea boats, or, as in destroyers, from any convenient position along the ship's side.

Leadsmen's aprons are supplied made of a band of sword matting, with a canvas flap and are secured to the stanchions in the chains.

The leadsman stands on the platform outside the berthing rails and leans his whole weight against this apron, the canvas keeping his legs dry.

The leadsman, on going into the chains, must:

(1) Put on his cap securely, chin-stay down.

(2) Remove his knife and lanyard.

(3) See the apron properly secured.

(4) See the end of the lead line is made fast.

(5) See that the becket is in good condition.

(6) See that the line is clear.

The lead is always hove in the direction in which the ship is moving.

Ease the lead down towards the water until the amount of scope is out—*i.e.*, the distance from the lead to the hand, generally 2 to 2¼ fathoms—then hold the line with a round turn round the hand and the coil in the other hand. Keep the body upright, face slightly in the direction the ship is moving, and rest against the top of the apron. Swing the lead as an ordinary pendulum, to obtain impetus, then swing it over the head in a circle by bending the arm smartly in at the elbow as the lead is rising and letting the arm go out again after the lead has r passed the perpendicular; after completing two or three circles slip the line after the lead has passed the water and before it comes to the horizontal, easing the coil out from the other hand; when it has run out as far as it is going, gather in the line with both hands, and obtain an up and down sounding as the ship passes the lead.

In shallow water, or if the ship is moving very slowly, greater accuracy is ensured and time is saved by using only the underhand swing. Many skilled leadsmen always employ this method instead of swinging the lead over the head.

To haul in the line. The line is always hauled in with the right hand under and the left hand over, so as to make a right-handed coil and prevent its kinking.

Calling Soundings

If the depth of water obtained corresponds with any of the marks on the line the leadsman calls, 'By the mark 5,' 'By the mark 7,' etc. If it corresponds with what he judges to be a deep, he calls, 'deep 6,' 'deep 8,' etc. If a quarter or half a fathom more than a mark or a deep he calls, 'and a quarter 7,' 'and a quarter 8,' etc., or 'and a half 7,' 'and a half 8,' etc. If a quarter of a fathom less than a mark or a deep, then he calls 'a quarter less 7,' or 'a quarter less 8,' etc.

Care should be taken on no account to over-estimate the depth of water, and it is customary to call a quarter of a fathom less than the actual soundings.

The depth of the water in daylight is seen by where the water cuts the lead line when the lead is at the bottom and directly under the leadsman; but after dark by deducting from the nearest mark to the hand the distance from the top of the apron to the water's edge. This distance is called the 'drift.'

When soundings are required at very short intervals a second man is generally placed in the chains to assist in hauling in the line.

The lead should always be kept on the bottom when a ship is getting under way, and on anchoring directly the ship stops or goes astern, and the leadsman should report directly the ship moves either ahead or astern or ceases to move. This is essential in the dark.

Lead lines must be measured when wet, and marked from the bottom of the lead. Before fitting a new line it should be stretched thoroughly by towing astern.

BOAT LEAD AND LINE

The weight of the lead is 7 lb., and it is of leg-of-mutton shape. The line is generally made of 2½-lb. line, and is about 10 to 12 fathoms long. It is marked in feet up to 3 or 4 fathoms, after that in fathoms, in the same way as the hand lead.

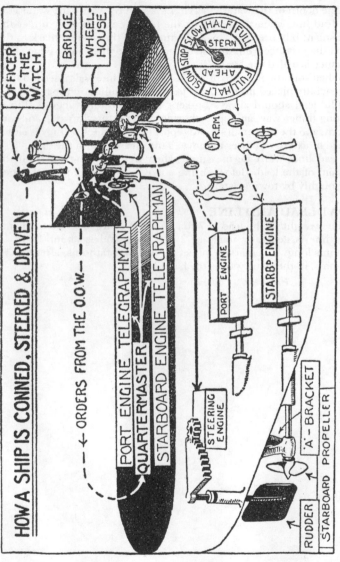

HOW A SHIP IS CONNED, STEERED & DRIVEN

BRIDGE

WHEEL-HOUSE

OFFICER OF THE WATCH

R.P.M.

STOP · SLOW · HALF · FULL
ASTERN
AHEAD
FULL · HALF · SLOW

← ORDERS FROM THE O.O.W. →

PORT ENGINE TELEGRAPHMAN

QUARTERMASTER

STARBOARD ENGINE TELEGRAPHMAN

PORT ENGINE

STARBD ENGINE

STEERING ENGINE

'A' - BRACKET

RUDDER

STARBOARD PROPELLER

Fig. 17

CHAPTER III
STEERING THE SHIP

HOW A SHIP IS STEERED

The Officer of the Watch stands on the **fore-bridge** conning the ship. He gives steering orders direct to the man at the wheel, usually by voice pipe, who repeats them and turns the wheel as ordered. The wheel sets the steering engine in motion, which turns the rudder, and the rudder turns the ship. (In small craft the wheel may work the rudder through direct gearing.)

The wheel indicator in front of the wheel shows how many degrees the rudder has turned. The greater the angle (up to 35 degrees) presented by the rudder to the fore and aft line, the quicker will the ship swing, and the smaller will be her turning circle, just like a car. Unlike a car, however, the ship will continue to swing some time after the wheel is put back amidships, so that when she is approaching the desired course the wheel must be put the opposite way for a time, until the swing is checked.

Ships can be steered on a straight course by means of the compass. a glass-topped bowl in which is suspended a round card, called the compass card. A line is drawn to the edge of the compass card, marked 'North,' and the compass is so made that the card will always remain stationary whenever the ship turns, with this 'North' line pointing towards the north. This is achieved either by small magnets attached to the card or by having the card connected to a large gyroscope fixed low down in the ship.

A gyro compass card will be marked 0° for north, 180° for south, 270° for west, and so on, up to 360°. For example, south-east will be 135°. (See Fig. 18.)

A magnetic compass card is divided on the outer edge into 360°— that is, into four quadrants of 90° each, north and south being marked 0°, and east and west 90°, e.g., south-east will be S.45° E. (See Fig. 19.)

The 'points of the compass' are no longer engraved on the magnetic compass card, but are still used to indicate the general direction of the wind, or of the bearing of an object. It will be seen from the accompanying sketch that each quadrant is divided into eight equal parts, the division marks being called 'points,' each having a distinctive name given to it. (Fig. 20.)

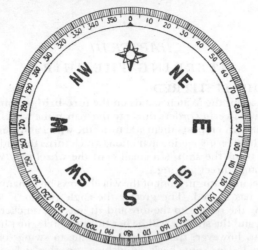

Fig. 18   Gyro Compass Card.

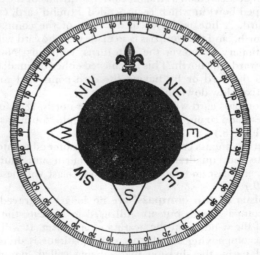

Fig. 19   Magnetic Compass Card.

FIG. 20

S.	W.	N.	E.
S. by W.	W. by N.	N. by E.	E. by S.
S.S.W.	W.N.W.	N.N.E.	E.S.E.
S.W. by S.	N.W. by W.	N.E. by N.	S.E. by E.
S.W.	N.W.	N.E.	S.E.
S.W. by W.	N.W. by N.	N.E. by E.	S.E. by S.
W.S.W.	N.N.W.	E.N.E.	S.S.E.
W. by S.	N. by W.	E. by N.	S. by E.
W.	N.	E.	S.

The **lubber line** is a line drawn on the bowl of the compass, level with the edge of the card, representing the ship's head. It is important **to remember that the lubber line moves with the ship, as she turns, while the card itself remains stationary.**

The man at the wheel, when ordered to steer a compass course, keeps the lubber line constantly opposite the desired point on the compass card by turning his wheel to port or starboard, *moving* the lubber line.

HOW A SHIP IS DRIVEN

The ship's engines may be steam, diesel, or internal combustion engines, turning various types of fuel into energy. Each engine is connected to a shaft which runs out through a watertight gland, under water aft, and which is fitted with a screw propeller outside the ship. When a long length of shaft is exposed it must be supported by an 'A' bracket fixed outside the hull and holding the shaft in a bearing.

When the propeller is revolved by the engines, the ship is driven along. A ship may have one or more propellers. Besides driving the ship, two propellers are useful for manoeuvring her round in a narrow space.

The officer on the bridge gives orders to the **helmsman** or quartermaster for moving the engines, as well as for steering the ship. The helmsman repeats these orders, and they are repeated in turn by the men stationed with him in the wheelhouse at each engine room telegraph. These telegraph-men move their pointers to 'slow,' 'half,' or 'full speed,' 'ahead' or 'astern' as ordered. Below, the engine room staff see these orders repeated on their telegraph receivers, and control the speed of their engines by the throttles, or, if required, reverse them ahead or astern, by means of reversing gear.

The Captain of a ship gives his engineer officer directions regarding the meaning of 'full speed' when manoeuvring, or in emergency. He also fixes a number of revolutions for 'slow speed' and for the lower limit of 'half speed.' 'Half speed' begins a few knots faster than 'slow speed.' When all telegraphs are set to 'half speed' attention is paid to the *revolution indicator*, by which any number of revolutions per minute on all engines may be ordered. The revolution indicator is combined with the starboard engine telegraph. The normal position of engine room telegraphs in a ship on her course is, therefore, 'half speed ahead,' the revolution indicator being used to order the exact number of revolutions required so that the ship's speed through the water can be estimated, or so that small variations of speed can be made to keep at a distance from another ship when 'keeping station' on her.

STEERING

The **wheel indicator** is provided to show the man at the wheel how much the wheel has been turned. It is labelled starboard and port, coloured green and red, and always shows the number of degrees of rudder corresponding to the amount of wheel turned, from 5° to 35° each way.

There may be also a rudder indicator, an electrical instrument connected to the rudder, which gives the angle of the rudder itself at any moment, showing whether it is in step with the wheel indicator, or a mechanical repeat of the wheel indicator. These instruments are for the use of the officer conning the ship when he is not in sight of the wheel.

The great thing to remember is that the *top spokes of the wheel always move in the same direction as the ship's head.*

So that if you wish the ship's head to go to port the top spokes of

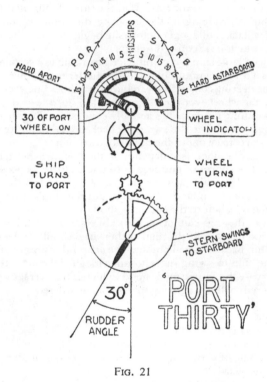

FIG. 21

the wheel must be moved to the left, and if to starboard the top spokes of the wheel must be moved to the right.

Steering by Compass

Remember that the lubber line represents the ship's head, and the compass card remains stationary while the ship swings round it.

If you wish the lubber line to go in any direction, move the top spokes of the wheel in that direction, and the lubber line (which is fixed to the ship) will swing round the card.

Hints on Steering

In a large ship, when the wheel is put over, the ship does not commence to swing for some time. If at the time of putting the wheel over the ship is swinging in the opposite direction, as sometimes happens, it will take still longer before she begins to swing back in the direction in which it is required to go.

When once a large ship has commenced to swing in a certain direction it takes a certain amount of opposite rudder to stop her again.

The art of steering consists in watching the lubber line very closely and putting the wheel over the instant the ship *starts* to swing off her course, not waiting until she has actually swung off. The wheel must be eased again as soon as the swing is checked, and opposite rudder used if she starts to swing in the opposite direction.

The amount of rudder used depends on the ship, her speed, and the weather, but **the secret of success is to use as little as possible.**

The best way to find when the ship has begun to feel the rudder put on is to look at the land or horizon and the ship's head will be observed to move, before the compass shows it.

In a seaway the ship cannot be kept always exactly on her course owing to wind or sea, but the man at the wheel should endeavour to swing the ship back an equal amount *the other side* of his course, not allowing the ship to swing more to one side of the course than the other, otherwise the course made good (which is the average of all the courses steered) will not agree with the course ordered.

Steering Orders

A wheel *order* consists of:

First, direction—port or starboard.

Second, rate of turn desired, given in degrees of rudder angle.

Thus: "Starboard 20!"

The *direction* comes first, and the wheel is immediately put over steadily to starboard, the helmsman *repeating* the order, "Starboard 20, sir," exactly as he hears it. When the wheel indicator reaches starboard 20 the helmsman stops the wheel at that point and *reports* "20 of starboard on, sir." The officer of the watch may then decide that the ship is swinging too fast, and will order "Ease to 15!" The helmsman repeats "Ease to 15, sir," and eases the wheel until the indicator points to starboard 15, when he *reports* "15 of starboard on, sir."

Note that a wheel *report* consists of—

(1) Angle of rudder on, first.

(2) Direction, port or starboard, second.

Approaching the new course the officer of the watch must check the swing of the ship. A point or two before reaching the new course, therefore, he will order "Midships!" The helmsman repeats: "Midships, sir," and having carried out the order reports: "Wheel's amidships, sir."

Even now the ship may be swinging too fast, and to 'meet her,' the officer of the watch will order "Port 10!" for as long as required to check the swing, then "Midships!" again when the ship's head is almost at rest, coming on to the new course. The O.O.W. must ensure that on no account is the ship allowed to swing past her new course since this would make it more difficult for ships astern to keep accurate station. As the lubber line of his standard compass arrives at the new course. the officer of the watch will order "Steady!" The helmsman will repeat "Steady, sir," noting the exact degree on his steering compass card opposite the lubber line at that moment, and will report the ship's head to the officer of the watch, *e.g.*, "North 26 east, sir," or "132 degrees, sir."

The order "steady" cancels any previous wheel order and requires the helmsman, until further orders, to use whatever wheel is necessary to keep the ship to the compass course ordered. After the order "steady" has been given, the ship is likely to swing a little one way or the other, and in order to make sure that the helmsman reported the correct course, the next time the ship is heading exactly N. 26 E. or 132 degrees, the helmsman reports "course north 26 degrees east" or "course 132 degrees." If the officer of the watch is satisfied he replies "Very good"; the helmsman continues to steer that course until further orders.

When the rudder of a ship is kept amidships, the ship, instead of steering a steady course, may show a tendency to wander away from it. When this happens it is caused by wind pressure against high superstructures, and by the effect of the waves on the hull forcing the ship's head either towards the wind, that is 'up into the wind,' or away from the wind, that is, 'falling off to leeward.'

To counteract this tendency the helmsman may have to keep a small angle on the rudder. This is called 'carrying rudder.' One ship may require rudder on one side to bring the ship's head up to the wind, because she tends to fall off; another ship, under the same conditions of wind and sea, may tend to fly up in the wind, and will require rudder on the other side to pay the ship's head off to leeward.

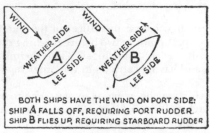

BOTH SHIPS HAVE THE WIND ON PORT SIDE:
SHIP A FALLS OFF, REQUIRING PORT RUDDER.
SHIP B FLIES UP, REQUIRING STARBOARD RUDDER

FIG. 22

The amount of rudder carried by a ship is always turned over by the helmsman to his relief.

The man at the wheel may or may not be in a position to see where he is going. Some steering positions are situated below, under armour. In a small ship, however, he will usually be able to see ahead, and if in company with other ships may be ordered to 'follow the next ahead.' In this case he will steer in her wake, using as little wheel as possible and keeping her masts, etc., in line with his own ship's stem. He must at all times be ready at the order "Steady!" to disregard the next ahead and steer by compass.

The helmsman **always** repeats all orders exactly as heard and reports when he has carried them out. The order "Hard a port" or "Hard a starboard" (*i.e.*, 35 degrees of rudder) is only given in an emergency. The normal order would be "Port 30," etc. Never force the wheel over. If it jams or gets stiff inform the quartermaster, who will tell the officer of the watch.

The helmsman's duty is to steer the ship under the supervision of the quartermaster. He is relieved every two hours, and on being relieved must inform his relief what the course is and what 'rudder' the ship is carrying. This two-hour turn of duty is called a 'trick.'

The telegraph-men do a similar '*trick.*' At sea only one man is usually required at the telegraph.

Helmsman and telegraphman are 'sea duty men,' and are detailed from the watch on deck. When closed up at their stations they must never carry steel, such as knives, keys, etc., which might affect the accuracy of the magnetic compass.

Special Sea Duty Men

These are special standing numbers who relieve the ordinary sea duty men in action or on entering and leaving harbour, etc. The chief quartermaster takes charge of the wheel, and the telegraphs are fully manned by special ratings.

THE RULE OF THE ROAD

The International Regulations for Preventing Collisions at Sea are printed in full in several publications, including the Admiralty Manual of Navigation, Vol. I., and the Admiralty Manual of Seamanship, Vol. I. **Before taking charge of even the smallest vessel under way it is necessary to have full knowledge of the thirty-one articles of the regulations. The following summary is not offered as a substitute.**

The 'Regulations for Preventing Collisions' at sea, commonly known as 'Rule of the Road,' are to the seaman what the 'Highway Code' is to the driver of a road vehicle. They tell him when he must give way to another vessel, and when he may expect the other vessel to keep clear of him. They require every vessel to carry lights at night of prescribed colour, arc of visibility, and range of visibility (on a clear dark night), to be fixed at certain heights and positions in the ship. In war-time it is often necessary to steam with no lights at all, but they are always kept ready. Dimmed lights can be shown when required, which are controlled by a dimming switch on the bridge.

Certain lights carried by vessels under way are designed to show approximately which way these vessels are heading. These are called **navigation lights,** and vessels showing such lights are able to estimate each other's position, course and speed with sufficient accuracy to take action in accordance with the regulations for preventing collision.

NAVIGATION LIGHTS FOR STEAM VESSELS
(see Articles 1, 2, and 10)

Steaming Light

One bright white light forward (*e.g.,* on the foremast) visible ahead to two points abaft each beam. A second steaming light may be carried, similar to the above, but fixed further aft and higher than the first light.

Bow Lights

(Sometimes called 'side-lights.') These are placed lower than the steaming lights. On the port side a **red** light shows from right ahead to two points abaft the port beam. A **green** light shows from right ahead to two points abaft the starboard beam.

Overtaking Light

All vessels must show a white light aft when being overtaken. When fixed, this light must show from right astern to two points abaft either beam, on about the level of the bowlights.

NAVIGATION LIGHTS FOR SAILING VESSELS
(see Article 5)

Sailing vessels and vessels in tow show bow lights and stern light only.

SPECIAL LIGHTS (see Articles 3 to 9 and 12 to 14)

Certain vessels whose freedom of manœuvre is affected by the work on which they are engaged, such as fishing, minesweeping, towing, laying telegraph cables, etc., or as the result of breakdown of engines or steering gear, such as vessels not under command, or aground in a fairway, show certain distinctive lights in addition to or in place of the ordinary navigation lights. By day such vessels hoist 'day marks,' *i.e.*, black shapes, for the same purpose.

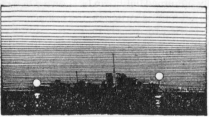

FIG. 23

Anchor lights (see Article 11)

All vessels at anchor or made fast to a buoy, etc., show a white light visible all round the horizon carried on the forestay, etc. Vessels exceeding 149 feet in length must show another similar light near the stern, at a lower height than the first light. Anchor lights are also called **riding lights.**

THE STEERING AND SAILING RULES (see Articles 17 to 27)

The steering and sailing rules direct that all steam vessels keep out of the way of sailing vessels, and that all vessels keep out of the way of a ship they are overtaking. They provide for practically all conditions of two vessels approaching, when risk of collision exists, the main principles being:

(1). That each captain is responsible for the safety of his own ship.

(2). That the ship directed to keep clear avoids crossing ahead of the other.

(3). That, broadly speaking, ships 'keep to the right.'

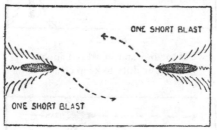

FIG. 24

'When both lights you see ahead
Starboard wheel and show your red.'

When two steam vessels are approaching one another end on, or nearly end on, each keeps to the right (*i.e.,* each ship alters course to starboard) (see Article 18).

FIG. 25

In narrow channels and fairways ships keep nearer to the bank which lies nearest to their starboard side, *i.e.,* they keep to the right (see Article 25).

STEAM VESSELS CROSSING

When two steam vessels are crossing so as to involve risk of collision, the vessel which sees the other on her own *starboard side* keeps out of the way (see Article 19).

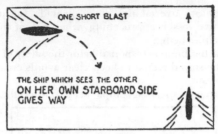

Fig. 26

If to your starboard red appear
it is your duty to keep clear.

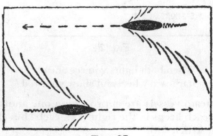

Fig. 27

When two ships are passing:
        Green to green, or red to red,
        Perfect safety—go ahead.

When the rules require one vessel to keep out of the way the other vessel is to keep her course and speed (see Article 21). The vessel which is directed to keep out of the way must avoid crossing ahead of the other (see Article 22).

When required to take action under the regulations vessels *in sight of one another* make clear their intentions by sound signals (see Article 28).

A steam vessel sounds on whistle or syren:
    1 short blast means, "I am directing my course to starboard."
    2 short blasts mean, "I am directing my course to port."
    3 short blasts mean, "My engines are going full speed astern."

FOG, MIST, SNOW, etc. (see Article 15 and 16)

In fog or thick weather all vessels, whether steam or sail, under way or at anchor or aground, are required to make distinctive sound signals to show where they are and what they are. For instance:

A steam vessel under way sounds *one* prolonged blast at intervals of not more than two minutes.

A steam vessel under way, but stopped and not moving through the water sounds *two* prolonged blasts at intervals of not more than two minutes.

A sailing vessel under way sounds, at intervals of not more than *one* minute, one blast when on the starboard tack, and *two* blasts when on the port tack, and *three* blasts when sailing with the wind abaft the beam.

All vessels at anchor ring the bell rapidly for five seconds at intervals of not more than *one* minute.

No officer can take charge of a watch at sea until he has thoroughly mastered the thirty-one articles in the Regulations for preventing collisions at sea.

CHAPTER IV

RIGGING

"Top hamper: *Necessary weight carried on deck or aloft, but which is an encumbrance at times"* ("Admiralty Manual of Seamanship," vol. i).

Weight aloft increases the rolling motion of a vessel. Too much weight aloft, as when too many men stand up together in a boat, will capsize her. The masts, spars, blocks and cordage which form the rigging of a warship are the minimum required to provide masts for W/T and flag signalling purposes and to carry lights. Masts are supported by 'standing rigging,' *i.e.,* shrouds and stays permanently set up in place.

The ropes and blocks provided for hauling are termed 'running rigging.'

EXPRESSIONS EMPLOYED IN HANDLING ROPES

To heave: to throw or pull on a rope, etc.

"Heave!": an order to give a strong pull together.

Heaving line: a length of light line having at one end a heavy knot to assist when the line is thrown; *e.g.,* thrown ashore, from a vessel coming alongside, to enable the end of a heavier rope hitched to the inboard-end of the line to be passed ashore.

To haul: to pull on a rope *by hand*.

"Avast hauling!": an order to stop.

To haul taut: to take the strain.

"Haul away!": an order to haul steadily until further orders.

To check: the reverse of 'haul.' The rope is steadily eased out, but held under control, keeping the strain on it.

To snub: to restrain suddenly a rope that is being checked.

"Well!": "Enough." The order to stop hauling or checking.

To hoist: to haul on a rope when a weight is to be *lifted*.

"Hoist away!": an order to hoist steadily until further orders.

"High enough!": an order to stop hoisting.

"Lower away!": an order to lower steadily until further orders.

"Avast lowering!": an order to stop lowering. ("Avast" = 'hold fast').

"Walk back!": an order to check by walking back with rope in hand.

Handsomely: slowly, with care. *E.g.,* 'Lower handsomely!'

Roundly: smartly, rapidly.

Hand over hand: hauling a rope quickly with alternate hands.

    Take a turn: to pass a turn round some fixture so that it takes the strain so long as the end is held, or 'backed up.'

Back up: to haul taut on the free end of a rope which is round a capstan or bollard. To assist those already detailed in performing some evolution.

Surge: to check a rope, easing the strain steadily, by letting the turns slip round the bollard, or capstan. To ease or render quickly.

Belay: to secure a rope with the strain on it to some fixture such as cleat or bollard.

Make fast: to secure a rope so that it will hold fast when the strain comes on it.

"Cast off!": an order to let go and free a rope which is belayed or made fast.

"Light to!": an order to fleet a heavy rope back along the deck to provide enough slack to belay it.

Marry: to join two ropes together side by side so that they are handled as one.

ROPES AND CORDAGE

    The length of rope is measured in fathoms (1 fathom = 6 feet). The size of a rope is measured by its circumference in inches.

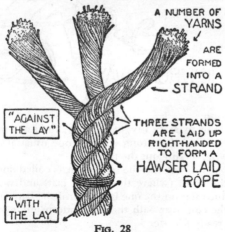

A NUMBER OF **YARNS** ARE FORMED INTO A **STRAND**

"AGAINST THE LAY"

THREE STRANDS ARE LAID UP RIGHT-HANDED TO FORM A **HAWSER LAID ROPE**

"WITH THE LAY"

Fig. 28

A rope is kept in a **coil** when not in use. (Seamen avoid using *both* ends of a coil at once for different purposes.) The part of a rope between the ends is called the **bight**.

Most service rope is **hawser-laid**, that is, formed of three strands **laid up**, or twisted, **right-handed** (*i.e.*, the strands twist away from the eye in a right-hand spiral). The strands themselves are twisted left-handed. The strands are formed of a number of **yarns**.

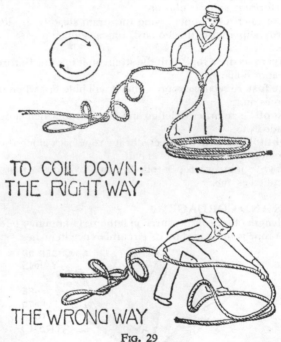

TO COIL DOWN:
THE RIGHT WAY

THE WRONG WAY

Fig. 29

To Coil a Rope

Because of this twist, or **lay**, of the rope, kinks and turns will form if the rope is coiled the wrong way. A rope must always be coiled down clockwise, 'taking out the turns.'

When a rope is made fast the remainder is coiled down as follows: Start with the bight (where the rope is fast) and work clockwise, laying each turn flat on the one below until the bare end is reached. Then turn the coil over with the end underneath, and the running part on top, ready for use.

HOW TO COIL A SMALL ROPE IN THE HAND

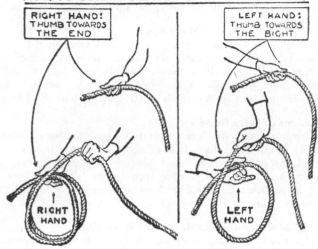

FIG. 30

The same care in controlling the rope must be taken when coiling a small line in the hand. When the coil is held in the left hand and formed with the right, the seaman always takes hold of the rope with his left thumb towards the bight. When the coil is held in the right hand and formed with the left, the right thumb points towards the end. The coils then form correctly of their own accord.

Whipping a Rope's End

When a length of rope is cut from the coil the strands tend to fly apart, or 'unlay.' All ropes' ends are therefore kept bound with twine to preserve the strands from fraying out. This is called whipping the rope's ends. The alternative is a back splice. A back splice will not reeve through a block.

Types of Rope

Hemp and **sisal** ropes are used for all general purposes in a ship, such as boats' falls, tackles, and rigging.

Coir rope (usually called 'grass line') is the weakest type of rope, and is unsuitable for use in blocks and tackles. It soon rots if stowed away wet. However, it is light enough to float and is very elastic, and is, therefore, useful for boat and rescue work. It is one-third the weight and one-quarter the strength of hemp rope, and looks rougher.

Advantages of Rope over Wire Rope

Rope yields to sudden jerking strains, and absorbs the shock, because it is fairly elastic. As it is not so easily damaged by kinks and sharp turns it lends itself to bends and hitches which would be impossible with wire rope. The same rope can be used for many purposes in turn because it is easily secured at any part of its length.

Advantages of Wire Rope

Wire rope is much stronger and lasts longer than hemp, sisal or coir ropes of the same size. It does not stretch and is less easily chafed. Consequently, it is used for all standing rigging, and wherever fixed lengths of flexible rope are required for running rigging. Wire rope is usually found fitted to the length required for one particular duty, with an eye spliced in each end.

Care and Maintenance of Rope and Wire Rope

All rope must be examined frequently for rot or damage, particularly when about to be used for lifting weights. Rot is detected by opening a strand. Damage and rot must be reported as soon as seen.

The life of hemp rope is shortened by:
 (1) Constant stretching at heavy duty.
 (2) Being allowed to chafe against sharp edges.
 (3) Stowing away wet, which quickly rots the rope.

The life of wire rope is shortened by:
 (1) Allowing kinks and turns to form in the wire.
 (2) Using a block, cleat, or bollard which is too small for the wire.
 (3) Allowing strands to be nipped or pinched out of shape.
 (4) Stowing away wet, which rusts wire strands and rots the hemp heart of the wire.

Ropes are therefore stowed away dry, and kept under a canvas cover. Wire ropes are dried, examined carefully for nips, parted strands, and rust, wiped over with linseed oil, and stowed on reels under waterproof cover. Machine oil will soon rot the hemp heart of a wire, and is worse than useless.

Precautions with Rope and Wire Rope

Never allow a rope to chafe against a sharp edge. **Fair leads** are provided at the ship's side to protect hawsers from chafe, and all fittings to which ropes are secured, such as **bollards** and **cleats**, are suitably rounded for the same reason. A seaman thinks out in advance where a rope is going to lead when it takes the strain, and if it is likely to rub against anything he will either shift his position or snatch on a **'leading block'** to hold the lead of the rope clear of the obstacle.

When the strain comes on a rope which is not properly under control, the situation may take a surprising turn. Never step inside a rope which is coiled or flaked down on the deck. Remember that a leading block may carry away, so stand on the right side of it. Never stand in the bight.

Before you put strain on a rope, think out what is going to happen at *both* ends of the rope. If you do not take charge of the ropes you use, they will soon take charge of you.

BENDS AND HITCHES

A **reef knot** is a method of bending together two short ends of rope of about equal size. It is familiar to everyone who has ever tied up a parcel.

The ropes are first crossed with the lay, and then against the lay.

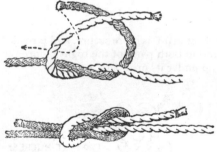

FIG. 31

Unless the ends are crossed opposite ways the result will be a 'granny,' which will slip.

Apart from the 'reef knot' the seaman only speaks of a **knot** when he is referring to one which is intended to remain permanently in a rope. Otherwise he **bends** one rope's end to another, and **hitches** a rope's end to a stay, or a spar, or a hook. He has evolved methods of doing this quickly in a variety of circumstances, in such a way that the rope holds under strain, yet can be quickly cast off when the strain is removed. This is particularly useful in the dark, or when the rope is wet and stiff.

A man is not a seaman unless he can make all the bends and hitches with his eyes shut, because these, as often as not, have to be made or cast off under water or in the dark.

A **sheet bend** secures a rope's end to a small ring, such as the ring of a hammock, or to the bight of another rope, or to the end of a rope of larger size. Pass the end through the loop in the bight, back round both parts of the bight and then across the loop under its own part.

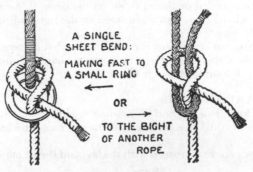

A SINGLE
SHEET BEND:

MAKING FAST TO
A SMALL RING

← OR →

TO THE BIGHT
OF ANOTHER
ROPE

FIG. 32

A 'double sheet bend' is more secure, and is made by taking one or more turns round both parts of the bight before the end is brought across the loop under its own part.

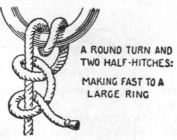

A ROUND TURN AND
TWO HALF-HITCHES:

MAKING FAST TO A
LARGE RING

FIG. 33

A **round turn, and two half hitches** secures a rope to a large ring, such as the ring of a buoy, or to a spar overhead. A full turn is taken round the ring or spar to the *right* of the bight. The end is then passed up over the bight from right to left and half hitched round the bight twice.

A **bowline** is a quick method of putting a temporary eye in the end of a rope, such as a hawser, or a line passed round a man working over the side. Two hands are required.

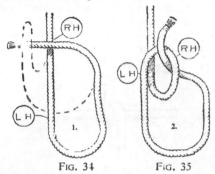

Fig. 34   Fig. 35

(1) **Left hand** takes weight of rope about 6 feet from the end, thumb towards the bight.

   Right hand takes rope 6 inches from the end, thumb towards the end.

   Right hand lays the end across the bight, holding the crossed parts together and taking the weight off the left hand.

   Left hand makes a loop over the end, holding the loop and releasing the right hand, which is now free to slip the end further through the loop.

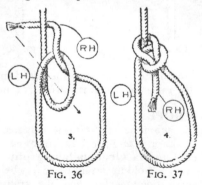

Fig. 36   Fig. 37

(2) **Right hand** pulls the end further through the loop held in the left hand, (3) dips it under the bight and (4) back through the loop along its own part.

A **running bowline** is made by pulling the bight through the eye of a bowline, to make a noose. It is useful when the bowline in a hawser is too small to fit over a bollard, when there is no time to make another. Never put a running bowline round a man's body.

A **clove hitch** secures a rope's end temporarily to a rail, etc., and is used to make fast the inboard end of a heaving line, or a hand lead line, or the line on a bucket, etc.

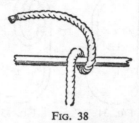

FIG. 38

Take the bight in the left hand, throw the end over the rail with the right hand, catch the end under the rail, pull it inboard to the *right* of the bight (1st half hitch).

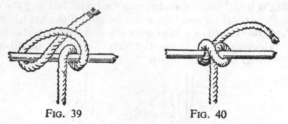

FIG. 39   FIG. 40

Pass it over round the rail again to the *left* of the bight and back outboard over the rail again under its own part (2nd half hitch).

BELAYING A ROPE

When a rope is taking the weight it is usually necessary to secure it taut with the strain on it and prevent it from easing back. When a rope is belayed round a **cleat, belaying pin** or **bollard**, it is therefore necessary to hold the strain while it is being belayed.

To belay a small rope to a cleat, keep the strain on the rope with the left hand while the right hand takes a turn under both arms of the cleat. Follow up the round turn by crossing further turns about alternate arms of the cleat in the form of a figure of eight. At least three turns are required. On no account should the rope be half-hitched round the cleat, or it will jam.

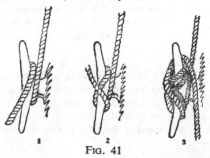

FIG. 41

To belay a rope round a single bollard take several turns round the bollard, then dip a loop of the bight under the standing part of the rope, throw this loop over the bollard, and haul taut.

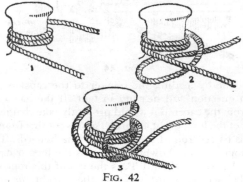

FIG. 42

To belay a rope round double bollards first haul taut the rope between the bollards, turn it round tie nearest and back between them

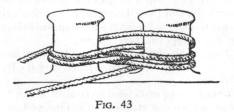

FIG. 43

and round the other bollard in the form of a figure of eight. Several turns are required. Stiff wire rope is prevented from springing off the bollards by means of a seizing round the crossed turns.

Cleats and belaying pins are unsuitable for wire rope because the wire will be forced into sharp bends or 'nips' when belayed.

PASSING A STOPPER

The strain on a large rope or hawser being too great to be held by hand, it is necessary to 'pass a stopper' to take the weight while the rope is being belayed. For instance, after sending a heavy hawser to a bollard on shore it may be required to heave in the slack by capstan, transfer the hawser to a bollard at the ship's side, and there belay it.

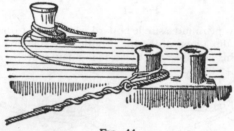

Fig. 44

This is done by leading the hawser to the capstan through the bollards in question and heaving in taut. If the hawser were now removed from the capstan it would promptly take charge, because of the weight of the long bight ashore. To prevent this from happening a stopper is passed round the hawser at the bollards. Take a short length of rope, make a bowline, and pass the loop over the bollard nearest the hawser, outboard. Pass the tail of this rope or 'stopper' over the hawser outboard towards the weight, *against the lay*, forming a half-hitch, then 'dog' it back (reversing the direction of twist) several turns *with the lay* round the hawser, and stop the end to the hawser. (If these turns are put on *against* the lay the hawser will slip through the stopper.) The stopper will then grip the hawser while it is being transferred from the capstan and belayed taut round the bollards. The stopper is then cast off.

With wire hawsers a chain stopper would be applied in a similar way, but in this case the half-hitch is taken *with* the lay and dogged *against* the lay.

A **chain check stopper** is used to control a wire being paid out where there is a convenient deck bolt. One end of the chain is secured; the other is passed through the eye of the deck bolt, round the wire and back through the deck bolt. Any strain put on this end of the chain, by means of a small purchase, or 'jigger,' will nip the wire against the deck bolt and so control its speed as it runs out.

Patent **steppers** and **nippers** are also supplied for controlling the movements of wire hawsers, especially when those hawsers are used in connection with anchor or towing work.

SPLICING ROPE

'Splicing' means joining two ropes end to end by interlocking the strands permanently together.

A **long splice** is used when the join is to be rove through a block, as a good long splice is the same size as the rope.

A **short splice** is simpler, but more bulky.

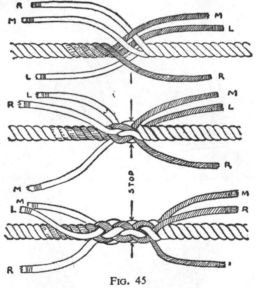

FIG. 45

To make a short splice in hemp rope unlay the three strands of each rope's end as necessary; then whip the ends of all six strands with a yarn, marry them together and put a stop round the fork. Tuck the three strands of one rope's end twice, as follows: Pass the left hand strand against the lay over the first strand next to it, and underneath the second strand, haul it into the lay of the rope, then enter the right-hand strand, and lastly the middle strand in a similar **manner** to the first, or left-hand strand. A **fid**, or wooden spike, is used to open the rope for tucking each strand. A steel marline spike is used for wire splicing. Haul the strands taut along the lay of the rope, and tuck all three strands once more as before. Cut the stop off the fork, and tuck the three strands of the other rope once, stretch the splice, whip all strands close up, and cut off the ends.

An Eye Splice

To make an eye splice unlay the three strands, farm the eye to the required size and tuck the middle strand through the top strand of the rope. Then tuck the left strand over the top strand and under the next strand.

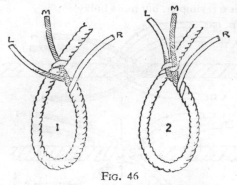

FIG. 46

Now turn the work over and tuck the right-hand strand under the strand not already used.

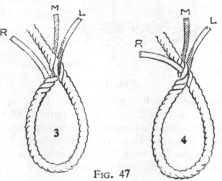

FIG. 47

Care should be taken to retain the lay of the rope in the last strand tucked, to enable it to lie closer.

Tuck all three strands a second time.

GEAR USED IN RIGGING

Standing rigging always stands permanently in place to support the masts and spars of a ship. The strongest *steel wire* rope is employed, of a type which does not bend easily. Each length of rigging wire is fitted to the exact length required with an eye spliced in each end holding a **thimble** or iron ring grooved on the outside to take the wire. The object of the thimble is to prevent the wire from bending round too sharply, and to protect the wire eye from chafe. These eyes can then be connected wherever required by **shackles**. Remember: 'Where there's a shackle there's a thimble.' A shackle is an iron 'U' formed into a 'D' by means of a bolt or **pin** which screws in place through the ends, or 'lugs,' of the 'U.'

The wire ropes supporting a mast are called **stays**. The strongest stays supporting the mast athwartships are called **shrouds**, while those supporting it in the fore and aft direction are fore stays and back stays. These stays are shackled to the deck at the ship's side and set up taut by rigging screws.

Spars

When a mast is small enough to be made in one piece it is called a **pole-mast**. Otherwise a **topmast** will be fitted at the head of the **lower mast**, and, if necessary, a **top gallant mast** at the head of the top mast. The shrouds support the lower mast at a point below its top or cap. Between this point and the cap is the lower **masthead**. The highest point of à mast is covered by a round wooden disc called a **truck**.

Yards are crossed on a mast for flag signalling ˙purposes, or to spread wireless aerials. The weight of a yard on a mast is taken by a chain sling; the yard-arms are held up level by wire **lifts** and squared back athwartships by 'braces.' Signal **halliards** for hoisting flags axe rove through small blocks along the yard; they are made of soft white hemp rope or sisal.

The **gaff** is the short spar which carries the ensign halliards; the lower end, at the 'throat,' rides on the after-side of a mast, while its after end, called the 'peak,' is triced up at an angle. (Warships wear their ensign in peacetime at an ensign staff right aft on the quarterdeck; in harbour they also wear a union flag at a 'jack-staff' right forward 'in the eyes of the ship').

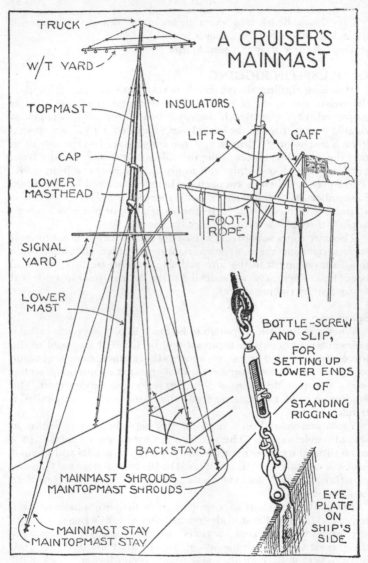

A CRUISER'S MAINMAST

TRUCK

W/T YARD

TOPMAST

INSULATORS

LIFTS

GAFF

CAP

LOWER MASTHEAD

FOOT-ROPE

SIGNAL YARD

LOWER MAST

BOTTLE-SCREW AND SLIP, FOR SETTING UP LOWER ENDS OF STANDING RIGGING

BACKSTAYS

MAINMAST SHROUDS
MAINTOPMAST SHROUDS

EYE PLATE ON SHIP'S SIDE

MAINMAST STAY
MAINTOPMAST STAY

Fig. 48

A **boom** is a horizontal spar, one end pivoted to the ship's side, or to a mast, the other end topped up level by a lift, or 'topping-lift.' A boom may be rigged outboard for securing ships' boats alongside clear of the ship, or to hold clear the wire of a sounding machine, etc. The ropes holding it in position are called **guys**.

Running rigging includes all ropes, wires, etc., employed aloft which work through blocks, or which are used to shift the position of spars and other gear. Flexible steel wire rope (F.S.W.R.) is used wherever a wire rope is to bend easily round the sheave of a block, etc. Flexible wire ropes contain more hemp and less wire than a rigging wire, and, in consequence, are less strong size for size.

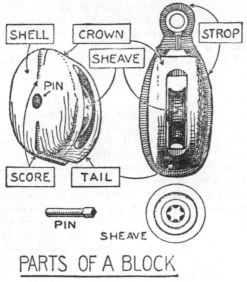

PARTS OF A BLOCK

FIG. 49

A **block** was originally a block of wood with a hole in it for a rope to reeve through. To save friction the hole was enlarged to take a pulley-wheel or **sheave**. Then the surplus wood was cut away from the outside of the block, leaving a wooden shell. This was grooved to take a rope strop spliced round the block to secure it in place as required. When the wooden shell split the block was useless. The next improvement was the 'iron-bound block' in which the strop or hook was riveted to an iron case carrying the sheave and its pin, the wooden shell serving to stiffen the case. To-day the larger modern blocks are made of metal, and friction is further reduced by roller-bearings between the sheave and its pin.

Purchases

A single **whip** is a rope rove through a single block overhead to hoist a weight. No power gained.

A **purchase** is a combination of blocks in a tackle where power is gained.

A **fall** is a rope rove through the blocks of a purchase.

A **pendant** is a flexible wire rope shackled to the moving block of a purchase to join it permanently to its work.

A **tail** is a rope spliced to the upper block of a purchase, by which it may be hitched temporarily to a beam or a spar, or a rope.

A **double whip** is the simplest form of purchase where a rope is rove through two single blocks, the end of the fall being secured to the upper block. Power gained—double. As this end of the fall does not move it is called the standing part of the fall; the other end is the **hauling part.**

Purchases may be rigged to gain further power by making use of blocks having two or more sheaves.

Much of the power gained in a purchase is lost in friction. Power gained must not be confused with the strength of a purchase. The size of rope employed (and consequently the size of the blocks), must be chosen to suit the weight to be lifted.

The purchases or tackles commonly carried about a ship for general purposes are the luff, the jigger, and the handy billy.

A **luff** is used wherever a heavy pull is required—two hook blocks (one double and one single) and 2½–3½ inch rope. A luff can usually be recognised by the standing part, which is passed through a becket in the strop at the tail of the single block and spliced round the strop at the neck of it. Power gained 3 or 4 times.

A **jigger** is a smaller cackle for general use, fitted either with hook blocks as in a luff, or with a tail on the double block instead of a hook (tail jigger). The standing part of the fall is spliced into the strop of the single block.

A handy billy is a small tackle for general purposes.

'Two blocks': A purchase is said to be two blocks when both blocks are hauled up together and touching.

'Overhaul': A purchase is said to be 'overhauled' when the two blocks are separated further apart by easing out the fall.

'Round up': The opposite to 'overhaul.'

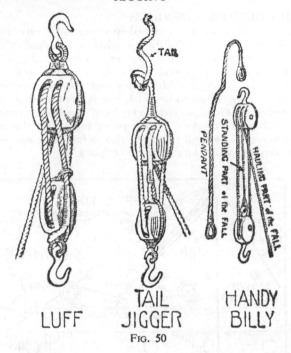

LUFF   TAIL JIGGER   HANDY BILLY

Fig. 50

Orders for working a Derrick

	Single Whip	*Purchase*
To hoist the weight:	"Hoist away."	"Up purchase."
To stop hoisting:	"High enough."	"High enough."
To lower the weight:	"Lower away."	"Lower purchase."
To stop lowering:	"Avast lowering."	"Stop purchase."
To work guys:	"Tend your guys."	
	"Haul away [or check] your fore [or after] guy."	

	Topping lift
To raise the head of the derrick:	"Up topping lift."
To lower the head of the derrick:	"Lower topping lift."
To stop raising:	"High enough topping lift."
To stop lowering:	"Avast lowering."
	(*Single Whip, Light, with no load*)
To raise the hook quickly:	"Up whip."

THE RIGGING OF A DERRICK

A derrick is simply a boom topped up at one end to carry the block of a whip or purchase for hoisting weights, like a crane. The lower end, or 'heel,' pivots on the foot of a mast or the side of a superstructure; the upper end, or 'head,' is topped up by another purchase called a 'topping lift' at any angle desired to plumb the purchase over the weight to be lifted. The head of the derrick is also prevented from being lowered too far by a 'standing topping lift,' a wire permanently connected to a point higher up the mast or superstructure. The head of the derrick is hauled round sideways and steadied as required by ropes called 'guys.'

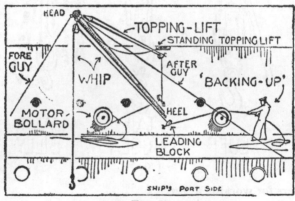

Fig. 51

The weight to be lifted may be hooked on and hoisted either by a single whip or by a purchase; the whip or fall is led through a leading block near the heel of the derrick and can be brought to the drum of a winch or hauled by hand. The working topping lift can also be brought to a winch or hauled by hand.

PARAVANES

The paravane, or 'P.V.' is used to sweep aside and cut the mooring wires of moored mines lying in the path of a ship so as to prevent the mine from striking the ship's hull. P.V.s offer no protection against either the magnetic mine or the acoustic mine, both of which are disposed of by other means.

1. MINES AHEAD: OUT P.Vs.
2. TOWING WIRE OF PORT P.V. CATCHES MINE MOORING.
3. MOORING SLIDES DOWN P.V. TOWING-WIRE INTO JAWS OF THE CUTTER.
4. RELEASED MINE FLOATS TO THE SURFACE.

FIG. 52

The floating moored mine is held below the surface by its mooring wire to the 'sinker' on the sea bottom. The P.V. is a kind of underwater kite, which is so constructed that when towed from a ship's bows it turns on its side and rides out away from the ship, presenting a taut horizontal towing wire which will catch any vertical mooring wire it may meet. The mine mooring wire slides down the towing wire, away from the ship, until it drops into the jaws of the cutters on the P.V. With its mooring severed, the mine rises to the surface clear of the ship.

To get out P.V.s, and to recover them, requires special gear and good seamanship. A full description of the methods of using P.V. gear will be found in Chapter IV of the "Admiralty Manual of Seamanship," Vol. ii.

CHAPTER V
ANCHORS AND CABLES

THE USE OF ANCHORS

When a ship is to remain for any length of time in one place she must be prevented from drifting away on wind and tide by means of anchors and cables.

The three principal ways of doing this are:

(1) Letting go a **single anchor.**
(2) Letting go **two** anchors and **mooring** between them.
(3) Securing to a **buoy** which has its own moorings permanently laid down.

HOW AN ANCHOR HOLDS

A ship cannot anchor where the water is too deep. It is not only a question of whether the cable is long enough to reach the bottom; it is important to remember that the anchor is designed:

(1) To hook firmly into the sea-bed when the cable is pulling straight along the ground from the anchor.
(2) To break out of the ground easily when the cable is pulling from above.

Therefore, the anchor will only hold so long as part of the cable nearest to it is lying along the bottom, exerting a straight pull. The more cable a ship has out the less likely is she to drag; in fact, a ship is really 'anchored' by her cable.

TYPES OF ANCHORS

There are two distinct types of anchor.

(1) Stocked anchor, usually known as Admiralty pattern. This type has been superseded except in some ship's boats by

(2) Stockless anchors which vary in pattern and shape, are found in most craft for all anchor work. Ses diagram for typical patterns of above.

CABLES

Anchor cables vary from chain in the case of large ships, down to **hemp** in the case of small boats.

Chain cable is composed of wrought-iron links. In the larger-sized

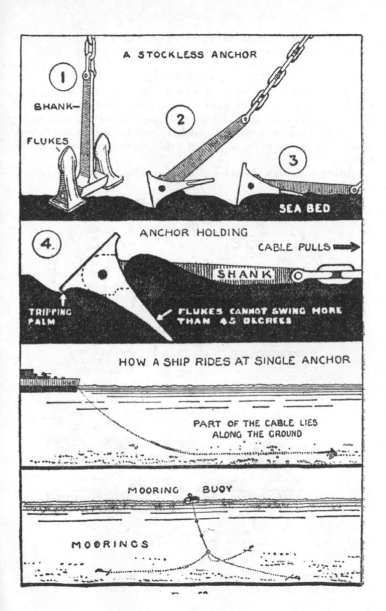

A STOCKLESS ANCHOR

① SHANK

FLUKES

②

③

SEA BED

④ ANCHOR HOLDING

CABLE PULLS →

SHANK

TRIPPING PALM

FLUKES CANNOT SWING MORE THAN 45 DEGREES

HOW A SHIP RIDES AT SINGLE ANCHOR

PART OF THE CABLE LIES ALONG THE GROUND

MOORING BUOY

MOORINGS

cables these links are studded to prevent kinking. The size of all chain cables is measured by the diameter of the metal forming the link.

Cable is supplied in shackles.

The length of a shackle of cable is 12½ fathoms.

This must never be confused with a cable's length—a term that indicates a distance of 200 yards. The number of shackles of cable supplied to ships varies, but for general purposes the average is about 12 shackles for each main ship's anchor. Merchant ships and fishing vessels use the term 'shackles' of cable to denote lengths of 15 fathoms.

Joining Shackles. Shackles of cable are joined together by joining shackles.

A JOINING SHACKLE OF THE LUG-LESS TYPE

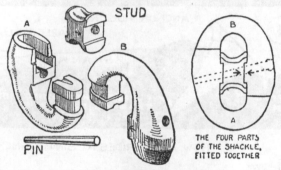

Fɪɢ. 54

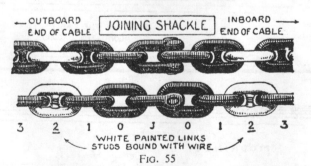

Fɪɢ. 55

Marking of Cables. It is essential, of course, that when anchoring a ship the shackles of cable must be marked so that it acan be seen at a glance how many shackles of cable have passed through the hawse pipe. The method of doing this is to mark the appropriate studded link either side of the joining shackle by painting these links white and binding wire round the studs (see diagram).

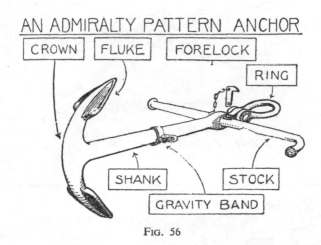

AN ADMIRALTY PATTERN ANCHOR

CROWN | FLUKE | FORELOCK

RING

SHANK | STOCK

GRAVITY BAND

Fig. 56

ANCHOR WORK FITTINGS

Cable Locker. A compartment between decks in which the cable is stowed.

Cable Clench. Secures the inboard end of the cable in the locker to the ship.

Cable Slips. There are various occasions when it is necessary to make sure a cable will not move. Slips are a form of clasp which are designed for this purpose.

Slips used in cable work are known as Blake slips.

The tongue of the slip does not go through the link of a cable but across it (see diagram).

The length of chain securing the Blake slip to the ship sometimes has a bottle screw inserted in it.

This permits the length of this connecting chain to be altered to suit requirement. A Blake slip so fitted is known as a Blake screw slip.

Blake slips are to be found on the forecastle and adjacent to cable lockers. The latter are known as riding slips.

BLAKE SLIP

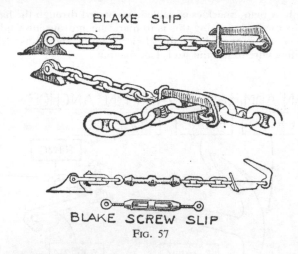

BLAKE SCREW SLIP

Fig. 57

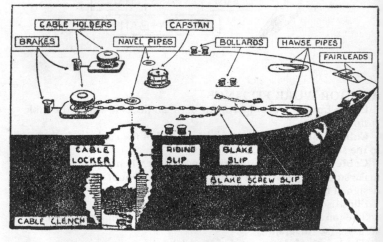

Fig. 58

THE LEAD OF CABLE

When a ship is anchored the cable of the bower anchor comes inboard on to the forecastle through a **hawse pipe**, and down through a hole in the deck known as a **navel pipe** to a compartment between decks called the cable locker, where the extreme end of the cable is fecured.

WINCHES, CAPSTANS, AND CABLE-HOLDERS

These are all power driven and designed for heaving in cables. Small vessels use a winch having its turning mechanism on deck. Larger warships use capstans or cable holders worked by mechanism placed between decks. Capstans and winches are constructed so as to serve a dual purpose in that they can be used for either chain cables or hawsers; they can generally be worked by power or hand.

A cable holder, as its name implies, is a form of capstan used for cables only.

Big ships are supplied with a cable holder to each cable, as well as a centre-line capstan for general purposes.

PRINCIPLES OF ANCHOR WORK

In all ships the main principles of anchor work are the same:
  (1) Cable must never be allowed to pile up on to the anchor when it has reached the bottom.
  (2) The anchor cannot be expected to hold unless part of the cable is pulling along the bottom.
  (3) Slack of cable on deck cannot be handled until the strain of the cable has been taken on a slip or similar device.
  (4) While the ship is riding to an anchor the cable must be secured inboard to bitts or cable holder, which are designed to be of sufficient strength to bear this strain.
  (5) The cable may part if subjected to sudden jerks or unfair strains, such as occur when it is hove round a sharp bend such as the stem of a ship or the wrong side of a hawse pipe.

SECURING ANCHOR AND CABLE FOR SEA

The ring of the anchor is lashed to eye bolts either side of the hawse pipe. The bight of cable is lashed down. Cable holder disconnected, brake on. Navel pipes plugged and covered. A bar is placed through the body of the Blake slip screw and lashed in place to prevent it easing back.

VARIOUS TERMS USED IN CABLE WORK

Anchor dragging: An anchor is said to be dragging when it is not holding in the ground. This is dangerous.

Come to: to anchor. A ship is said to have 'come to' when her way is stopped, and she is riding by her anchor and cable.

Veer cable is to pay or ease out a cable by turning the cable holder or capstan under full control of the turning mechanism.

Heave in cable is to heave in steadily by turning the cable holder or capstan.

Surge is to allow a cable or hawser to run out by by its own weight or by the strain on the outboard end. A hawser slipping round the barrel of a capstan is said to 'surge.'

Snub: to arrest the cable suddenly by applying the brake.

To bring to is to pass a cable round a capstan or cable holder, winch, etc., ready for working. It is always brought to with the studs or pins of joining shackles lying the same way as the barrel spindle, *e.g.*, upright, when brought to a cable holder or capstan.

Scope of cable: The length of cable paid out when a ship is riding at anchor.

Warping: moving a ship by means of hawsers.

Kedging: moving a ship by means of small anchors and hawsers.

Moorings are two or more anchors laid down with large chains which are brought to a central ring for a ship to secure to. A pendant is attached to the centre of the moorings, having a ring at the upper end to which a ship can shackle her cable. When no ship is secured to the moorings the weight of the pendant is taken by a buoy (see sketch).

Foul berth: when a ship has not room to swing.

Grow: A cable is said to grow in the direction in which it is lying. When the captain asks, "How does the cable grow?" the cable officer on the forecastle indicates the direction with his arm.

Shortening in cable: to heave in a certain portion of it.

Short stay: The cable is said to be at short stay when hove close in, but not up and down.

Up and down: The cable is said to be up and down just previous to the anchor being aweigh.

Anchor aweigh: The anchor is said to be aweigh as soon as it is broken out of the ground.

Hove in sight: The anchor is said to be hove in sight as soon as it can be seen when weighing. It is reported **'clear anchor'** when it is seen to be hanging fairly by the ring, or 'foul anchor' if the cable is round the anchor.

SECURING A SHIP TO A BUOY

As a ship at single anchor takes up a lot of room when she swings to the tide, a number of permanent moorings are laid down in certain harbours, with the object of saving space. Ships are secured by their cables to these moorings instead of using their own anchors. In very crowded harbours it may be necessary to moor vessels head and stern between two buoys, where they occupy still less room.

When securing to the ring of a mooring buoy, a **picking-up rope** is used. This is a wire hawser having a strop and a spring hook shackled

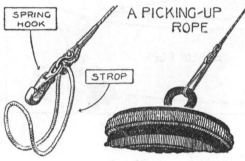

FIG. 59

to the eye. On arrival at the buoy the strop is passed through the ring and looped back over the hook. The ship can then be hauled close to the buoy by the picking-up rope brought to the capstan.

During the approach to the buoy the cable has been parted; the anchor being previously catted, or hung out of the way. A shackle large enough to take the ring of the buoy is then joined to the end of the cable, which is hauled out through the hawse pipe and lowered within reach of the buoy. When the cable has been shackled on to the ring of the buoy it is hove taut so that the picking-up rope may be cast off.

The length of cable between hawse pipe and buoy is called the **bridle**. Heavy ships sometimes require two bridles.

A SHIP LEAVING A BUOY

Before the cable can be unshackled from the buoy the eye of a wire hawser, called a **slip rope**, must be passed through the ring of the buoy and back to a slip. The other end of the wire is hauled taut and belayed round a bollard. Cable is then veered until slack enough to unshackle from the ring of the buoy, the ship meanwhile riding by the slip rope.

The slip rope is not left in position long enough to be damaged by chafing on the ring of the buoy.

When the ship is to proceed the slip is knocked off and the slip rope hauled inboard. The ship is then under way.

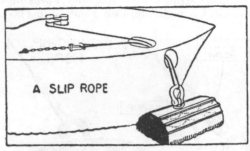

A SLIP ROPE

FIG. 60

Reeving a Slip Rope

The cable is first hove in at short stay.

A slip rope can then be passed out through a fairlead or through the hawse pipe. In ships with a pronounced flare, or overhang of the bows, the latter is preferable, since it brings the ring of the buoy closer to the cable end.

Precautions with Wire under Strain

When a wire under heavy strain parts, or is slipped, the ends tend to fly back in the line of the strain. It is therefore advisable to keep always out of the direct line of the strain, whether on the forecastle or lying off in a boat while the picking-up rope is hauling the ship to the buoy.

SECURING A SHIP ALONGSIDE

When depth of water and space alongside permits, a vessel in harbour may secure to a jetty.

Alongside a jetty provision must be made—

    (1) For the rise and fall of the tide.

    (2) For the alternate strains of the flood and ebb streams.

    (3) For wind and tide effects tending to move the ship away from the jetty.

    (4) For wind and tide effects tending to force the ship against the jetty.

A ship is therefore secured by means of hawsers to bollards on shore according to a definite plan, and is protected from damage against the jetty by **fenders** carried in the ship, or by **catamarans**, which are long rafts of timber moored alongside for the purpose.

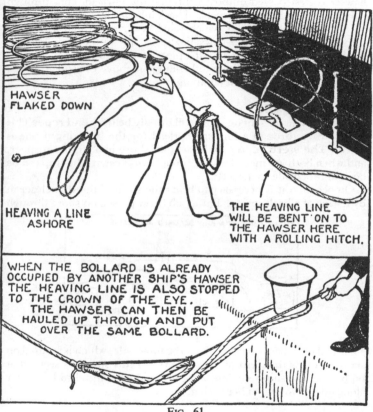

HAWSER FLAKED DOWN

HEAVING A LINE ASHORE

THE HEAVING LINE WILL BE BENT ON TO THE HAWSER HERE WITH A ROLLING HITCH.

WHEN THE BOLLARD IS ALREADY OCCUPIED BY ANOTHER SHIP'S HAWSER THE HEAVING LINE IS ALSO STOPPED TO THE CROWN OF THE EYE. THE HAWSER CAN THEN BE HAULED UP THROUGH AND PUT OVER THE SAME BOLLARD.

FIG. 61

Preparing to Come Alongside

When it is known which side of the ship is to come to the jetty, fenders are got ready on that side, hawsers flaked down for running, and **heaving lines** coiled down ready for coming alongside.

If the ship cannot be manoeuvred close enough with safety, hawsers are sent away in boats to be secured on shore; otherwise they may be passed to men ashore by heaving lines. The ship's end of a heaving line, after the other end has been caught by a man on shore, is bent on to the hawser clear of the eye, above the splice; this allows the line to be freed while the eye is fast round a shore bollard. The hawser is first passed outboard through the fairlead, etc., through which it is to ride, and the eye laid back inboard over the rails.

In the case of a hawser which must be rove through a ring, or through the eyes of other hawsers already fast to the same bollard, the heaving line is stopped with a piece of yarn to the crown of the eye of the hawser in addition to bending on above the splice. It will then haul through without jamming.

Coming Alongside

The first hawser sent on shore will usually be the **head rope**. This will be rove through a forward fairlead (or the bull ring if one is fitted). **The stern rope** may be sent on shore in a similar manner, and when both are made fast and brought *to* capstans the ship can be hove in broadside to the jetty.

On occasion it is necessary to bring the stern of the ship closer in by means of a back spring. This is a hawser passed on shore through

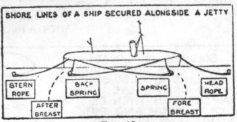

FIG. 62

a fairlead or bollards further aft on the forecastle, which is secured on shore towards the stern of the ship. When this spring is secured at both ends the ship's engines are moved slowly ahead to bring her alongside, pivoting on her spring.

Securing Alongside

The ship must be prevented from ranging ahead and astern along the jetty by long springs from forward in the ship to a position aft on shore, and vice versa; head rope and stern rope are fleeted as far ahead and astern as convenient and secured nearly taut. The longer these ropes are the less attention they will require when fully extended at low water. Care must be taken to see that they are long enough at low water, and when other ships are passing.

The ship must be prevented from moving away from the jetty by lines secured inboard abreast the positions where they are fast on shore. These are called **breast ropes**, and require constant attention while the tide is falling or rising.

The hawsers mentioned may be doubled and reinforced as necessary.

While alongside, a gangway is made in the berthing rails at the ship's side, through which is hauled a **brow**, or gang-plank, to bridge the gap between the deck and the jetty. The brow's lashings must be carefully watched to see that it is secure, yet allowed freedom of movement as the ship rises or falls with the tide.

LEAVING A JETTY

First, wires will be 'singled up,' leaving only those hawsers which are required to hold the ship in position, depending on state of weather and tide; the brow will be hauled on shore, and hands will close up at stations for leaving the jetty. In a small ship, if no one is available to cast off hawsers on shore, the last rope to be cast off (probably a spring or head rope) will be rove on a slip.

When ready to proceed the captain orders **"Let go, aft,"** the after spring and stern rope are let go, and reported, **"All gone, aft,"** and when hauled in clear of the screws, **"all clear aft."**

The captain may make use of the back spring to work the stern of the ship away from the jetty, after which he will order, **"Let go the spring."** When this has been cast off (**"All gone**, the spring"), and the ship is ready to move astern, he will order, **"Let go, forward."** The head rope is cast off, or slipped, and reported, **"All gone, forward,"** and when hauled clear inboard, **"All clear, forward."** Hands then fall in at stations for leaving harbour. One anchor is kept ready for letting go until clear of harbour, and all gear is secured for sea as soon as possible.

SECURING ALONGSIDE ANOTHER SHIP AT A BUOY

In this case no wires are affected by the tide's rise and fall. Fenders are so placed and wires rove that provision is made for ships to roll opposite ways without damage, while as little fore and aft movement as possible is permitted. Both ships will shackle a cable to the ring of the buoy, and when either unshackles to leave she reeves a slip rope.

PLACING FENDERS

Sharp corners cause the most damage unless fended. When your own ship has way on, have your fender slightly in advance of the point of impact, preferably in the way of a bulkhead or side frame (indicated by a row of rivets down the ship's side).

CHAPTER VI
BOATWORK

IT is an old service saying that a ship is known by her boats; therefore remember when away in a boat that you carry the credit of your ship with you, and strive to uphold it. A smart boat and seamanlike boat's crew is a sign of a smart and efficient ship. That is why service boats are kept as clean and shipshape as possible, why they are manned smartly, boat's crews dressed alike in every detail, and why they go about their business in a seamanlike fashion, without noise, fuss, or waste of time.

USES OF BOATS

Reference to the tables given on pages 280 to 285 (Chapter VIII) of vol. I "Manual of Seamanship," will show that a wide variety of different types of boat is carried in H.M. ships. Each ship, according to her size, carries a selection of these types, each type designed to carry out certain of the following functions:

(1) Patrolling.

(2) Laying out and weighing anchors and their cables, etc.

(3) Towing and landing armed parties, together with their guns and stores, etc.

(4) Ordinary harbour duties such as landing and embarking liberty men and stores, distributing correspondence to the fleet.

(5) Sea boats; specially seaworthy craft such as **cutters** and **whalers**, one of which is kept ready each side for lowering in the event of anyone falling overboard, or a boat being required quickly for any other purpose.

TYPES OF BOATS

The boats carried in warships are of two main types, namely, power boats and pulling boats.

Power boats may be divided into two main groups:

(1) High-speed craft, having very powerful engines compared with the weight of the boat. These are flat-bottomed (or 'hard chine') craft which are able to plane on the surface of the water as soon as a certain speed is reached

(2) Heavier and slower 'displacement' craft of 'round bilge' type, which are driven through the water instead of over the top of it.

Flagships carry a large steam boat or high-speed motor boat for the use of the Admiral. This boat is painted black with a miniature of the admiral's flag on either bow, and is called the **Admiral's barge**. When the barge is under way with the admiral on board she carries a small disc forward on which is painted the **Affirmative flag** (red with a white cross). When the admiral is not in the boat a disc painted with a **negative flag** (small black crosses on a white ground) is shown instead.

Pulling boats are all open boats propelled with oars. The larger pulling boats, such as **launches** and **pinnaces**, are nowadays fitted with motors in addition to oars, masts and sails. These are known, together with all power boats, as **boom boats**, because at sea they are stowed inboard amidships in a position formerly occupied by the 'booms,' *i.e.*, the stowage for spare spars, rafts and boats.

Smaller and more seaworthy types of pulling and sailing boats are cutters and whalers. These are used as sea boats. Cruisers and above sometimes carry a **gig** for the use of the captain; this boat is known as the **captain's galley**. The smallest pulling boats are called **dinghies**. These can be handled by one or two men under oars, sail, or outboard motor.

MANNING A BOAT

Properly handled, whalers and above are as safe in a gale of wind at sea as a battleship; carelessly or badly handled the same boat becomes dangerous in a flat calm.

Sea sense is soon acquired by a boat's crew, when it is seen that wind and tide accept no excuses, punishing all careless mistakes on the spot with extra work.

When manning a boat there are four important rules to be observed:
  (1) **Man your boat at the double.**
  (2) **Keep the boat trimmed.** Never crowd to one side or one end of a boat. Avoid jumping heavily and clumsily into her. Sit down at once where your weight will keep her trimmed level, and **don't stand up without orders.**
  (3) **Keep your hands off the gunwale.** Otherwise you will soon have your fingers crushed.
     Never allow ropes' ends, fenders, fittings, etc., to trail over the side.
     Never sit on the gunwale, or on ropes or gear which may be needed quickly.
  (4) **Keep silence.** A boat's crew must be constantly listening for orders. Safety depends on orders being instantly obeyed. This applies equally whether you are boat's crew or passenger.

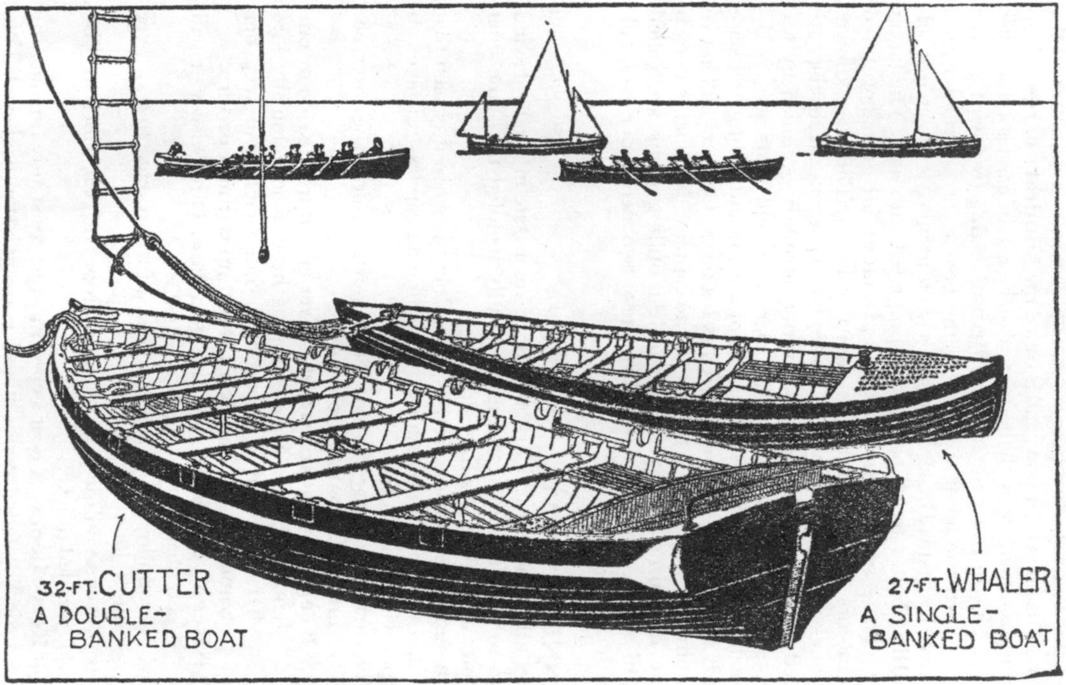

32-FT. CUTTER
A DOUBLE-BANKED BOAT

27-FT. WHALER
A SINGLE-BANKED BOAT

FIG. 63

PARTS OF A PULLING BOAT

The **hull** of a pulling boat is very like the hull of a ship except that her keel runs *outside* beneath the bottom of the boat from end to end. In a whaler the keel is continued up in the **stem post** and the **stern post**; all other boats are square sterned, the stern post carrying the **transom** or square end of the boat.

Across the keel, placed athwartships at intervals along the whole length of the boat are the **timbers** (frames or 'ribs'). The timbers are curved up on either side and are held in position inside the boat by long fore and aft strips of wood called **stringers**; they are covered over outside with planking. The plank edges may either overlap **(clinker built)**, or fit flush together **(carvel built)**. The top stringer at the edge of the boat's side is called the **gunwale**. A second stringer runs fore and aft about a foot below the gunwale each side supporting the ends of the **thwarts**.

The thwarts are wooden benches placed *athwart* the boat at intervals. The boat's crew sit on the thwarts, facing aft, with their feet braced against their **stretchers**, which are wooden foot-rests placed in the bottom of the boat at a convenient distance from each man. The foremost thwart is called the **bow thwart**, and the aftermost thwart is called the **stroke thwart**, because it is manned by the **stroke oar**, who sets the stroke for the rest of the crew. The space abaft the stroke thwart is the **stern sheets**. **Stern benches** are fitted each side and athwart the after end of the stern sheets. The thwarts are fitted rigidly to the sides and gunwales by wooden crooks or brackets called **knees**, thus helping to keep the boat in shape.

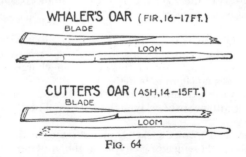

WHALER'S OAR (FIR, 16–17 FT.)
BLADE
LOOM

CUTTER'S OAR (ASH, 14–15 FT.)
BLADE
LOOM

FIG. 64

Single-banked and Double-banked Boats

When only one oar is manned at each thwart (*i.e.*, at alternate sides of the boat) the boat is said to be **single banked**. When an oar is manned at each side at each thwart she is said to be **double banked**. In single banked boats the weight and thrust of the oars is taken in metal **crutches**, which are shipped in socket plates fitted inside the gunwale. Crutches are always unshipped when the oars are not in use, except when a whaler is rigged as a sea boat. Double-banked boats have spaces cut in the washstrake (a thick plank fitted above the gunwale) called **rowlocks**, instead of crutches. Except when a cutter is hoisted as a sea boat rowlocks are always kept closed when not in use by shutters usually referred to as **poppets**.

The stern sheets are floored over with a grating under which, in the plank next to the keel (called the **garboard strake**), is a plugged hole in the bottom of the boat. The hole lets water out when the boat is hoisted, and the **plug** keeps it from getting in when she is afloat. The bottom of the boat beneath the thwarts is covered by **bottom boards**. Amidships, near each end of the keel, is fastened a link plate, to which one leg of the chain slings is hooked when the boat is hoisted. The other leg of the slings hooks into a ring bolt which is fastened through the stem post and stern post respectively.

DISENGAGING GEAR

The lower blocks of boats' falls are hooked on at each end of the boat to these slings. The boat is held level by steadying lines joining the slings to the sides of the boat.

It is absolutely necessary when lowering a pulling boat at sea, and when the ship has way on her, that both the falls should be disengaged from the boat simultaneously (so that the boat is level when she drops in the water); to effect this, ships are supplied with Robinson's disengaging gear.

Robinson's Disengaging Gear

This type belongs to the class in which the release of the boat remains under the control of the person in charge of her; but, therefore, makes no claim to be self-acting.

It consists of two tumbling blocks (H in sketches) so connected as to tumble simultaneously on the release of the line 'O' held by the coxswain.

It will be seen from the sketch that the toe on the ends of the tumbling hooks 'H' engages on a spur at the upper end of the lever 'K' so long as the **fore and after** 'M' is set up taut by the line 'O.' When the line 'O' is released, permitting the levers 'K' to swing outwards towards the ends of the boat, the tumbling hooks are free to swing up, thus releasing the boat's falls simultaneously at each

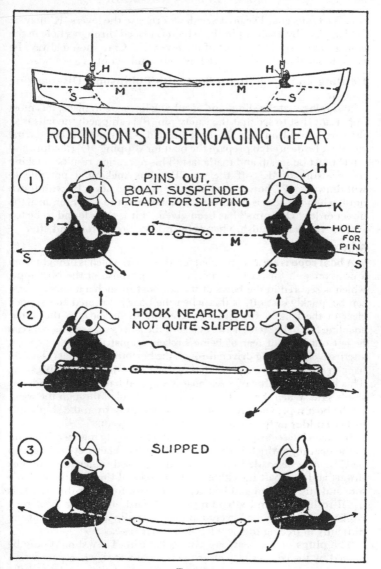

ROBINSON'S DISENGAGING GEAR

① PINS OUT. BOAT SUSPENDED READY FOR SLIPPING

H

K

HOLE FOR PIN

② HOOK NEARLY BUT NOT QUITE SLIPPED

③ SLIPPED

Fig. 65

end. As a safe-guard against accidental release the levers 'K' may be held in place by a safety pin 'P,' which is placed through a hole in the casing to prevent movement of the lever 'K.' Care should always be taken to see that these pins are free to be pulled out in a sea boat.

Hoisting and Lowering a Boat with Robinson's Disengaging Gear

Assuming that the slings and steadying lines are in place, it is most important first to see that the safety pin 'P' is shipped; the falls may then be hooked on and the boat hoisted. On reaching the davits, should it be desired to prepare the boat for slipping, 'O' (the fore and after) must be set up and made fast. This operation results in taking the pressure of 'K' off the pin 'P,' thus making it possible to withdraw 'P.' 'P,' however, should, in practice, never be withdrawn until, when the boat is being lowered, it is near the water, or until the direct order **"Out pins"** has been given. If it is then found to be too stiff to withdraw, midship hands bear down on the fore and after.

SEA BOATS

A **boat rope** is always provided for a sea boat, which is brought from a position well forward in the ship. The purpose of the boat rope, which is secured in the bows of the sea boat in such a manner that it can be quickly cast off, is that when the boat is lowered and slipped clear of the falls it will give steerage way to the boat in the water, enabling her to be steered away clear of the ship's side so that oars can be got out without fear of being broken against the ship's side, or, alternatively, of being driven through the bottom of the boat (as would happen if the boat were permitted to sheer in towards the ship's side). This is why the **tiller** of a sea boat is stopped hard over towards the ship's side. When the boat is slipped she is hauled through the water by the boat rope, and given an initial sheer away from the ship's side by her **rudder** until the stop is cut by the coxswain.

It is usual to secure it in the boat in the following manner. The end of the boat rope which is fitted to the boat has a large eye splice, or a bowline may be made in it. This end is passed under the foremost thwart and up abaft it, with a stretcher passed through the eye in a fore and aft direction and laid across the two foremost thwarts. It is usual to have a hand attending the inboard end of the boat rope whilst the boat is being lowered, prepared to slip it in the event of any difficulty in freeing the boat from the boat rope.

The **plugs** of sea boats are always kept in. They should only be moved by the coxswain to clear the boat of water, when permission to do so must be obtained from the officer of the watch, and the coxswain should remain in the boat until the plug is replaced. Extra life lines, one to each thwart, are placed on the jack stay between the davits; the falls are either flaked down clear for running, or are reeled up on two reels one to each fall. At the commencement of each watch the coxswain reports to the officer of the watch that his crew and lowerers are correct, the boat clear of water, plug in, *and the boat off the pins* (*i.e.*, the pins are free).

A sea boat when secured for sea should contain the following gear in addition to the ordinary boat's fittings:

Boat's bag.
This bag should contain the following:

Spunyarn.	Chisel.
Tallow.	Tommy.
Palm and needle.	Punch.
Marline spike.	Tingle (a copper sheet for
Twine.	temporarily repairing a hole).
Wax.	Copper nails.
Hammer.	

Note. The tools, tingle, and copper nails may be contained in a smaller bag called the carpenter's bag. A piece of felt or fearnought is included, to be placed over a hole under the tingle.

Sea boat's box.
This box contains:

4 Short lights.	12 Signal cartridges (6 green, 6 red).
1 Very's pistol.	

Barricoe (pronounced 'breaker') of water.
Boat's lead and line.
Lantern, candles and matches.
Lifebelts.
Hand axe.
Boat's signal book in cover, and semaphore hand flags and answering pendant.
Box of corned beef.
Box of biscuits.
Boat's compass (Patt. No. 183).

LOWERING A SEA BOAT
The lee boat is always the one to be lowered, and in a rough sea a good lee should be made, and if necessary oil used before lowering the boat.

On a sea boat's crew being called away, they man their boat instantly and put on their life-belts (one life-belt for each of the crew and the officer of the boat is always ready, lying across the thwarts). The oars are got ready on the gunwale, life lines crossed to prevent the boat surging in a fore and aft direction, and the crew on the inside stand by with stretchers ready to bear the boat off from the ship's side. *No one is to be abaft the after fall or before the foremost fall.* The bow and stroke oarsmen try the pins and ensure they are free, and the coxswain tends the fore and after which is belayed to a cleat aft. Sea boat lowerers, consisting of a leading hand and two seamen, are told off to each fall. The leading hand slips the gripes (with a hammer specially supplied for the purpose and secured to the davit by a lanyard) before starting the falls.

In the case of the sea boat being required to save life, the pipe **"Away lifeboat's crew"** may be substituted for **"Away sea boat's crew."**

Order	Action
"Away sea boat's crew, man the . . ."	Crew man the boat on the side piped and act as described above.
"Slip the gripes" . .	Gripes are slipped as described above.
"Turns for lowering" .	Lowerers take surplus turns off the staghorn.
"Start the falls" . .	As in harbour.
"Lower away" . .	As in harbour.
"Vast lowering" .	When the boat is low enough. Lowerers hold on to the falls.
"Out pins" . . .	Bow and stroke oarsmen take out the pins holding up their hands to signify completion. Coxswain then reports, "Pins out, sir."

Then, the first favourable opportunity, endeavouring to drop the boat on the top of a wave and not in the trough.

"Slip"	Coxswain lets go the fore and after, thus releasing the boat.

With the impetus given the boat by the ship, and the helm being over, she will sheer away from the ship. The crew at once get out their oars, the boat rope is slipped, and the crew give way. The general instructions on procedure in boats under oars apply to sea boats; oars should, however, never be kept tossed, but boated on arrival alongside.

HOISTING A SEA BOAT

A lee is formed by the ship if possible, and the falls well overhauled. The boat rope is made fast first. The boat is then hooked on, the foremost fall first and then the after one; life lines are crossed and stretchers prepared for use as in lowering. A second boat rope may be passed into the boat from well aft and secured in the stern. This boat rope should be kept manned inboard to prevent the boat scending forward; crossing the life lines is inadequate to stop a boat scending while being hoisted if the ship has much motion.

All the crew are hoisted in the boat, the falls being strongly manned so that the boat can be run up. In a seaway it is essential to get the boat clear of the water as soon as possible. Immediately the report "Ready in the boat" is received, the order "Haul taut, hoist away" should be given, all those in the boat not otherwise occupied taking their weight on the life lines.

When the boat is up and the falls secured, the crew take her weight off the pins by setting up the fore and after, and gripe her to; the life lines are left clear, the life belts replaced and the tiller stopped over towards the ship. The coxswain then reports to the officer of the watch that the boat is off the pins, and the falls clear for running.

LOWERING AND HOISTING BOATS IN HARBOUR

In normal weather in harbour it will not be necessary to slip a boat when lowered; if she is fitted with Robinson's disengaging gear the pins can be kept in and she can be lowered right down until waterborne and unhooked. Procedure for lowering is as follows:

Order	*Action*
"Away first cutter's crew, lower your boat	Crew fall in abreast their boat and are mustered by the cox-swain.
"Turns for lowering" . .	Bow and stroke oarsmen man the boat; see the life lines are clsar. Stroke oarsman puts the plug in, and hands take up position close to and between the falls, holding on to the life lines.

	The remainder of the crew divide themselves between the falls; take the falls in hand and remove outer turns ready for lowering.
"Start the falls" . . .	The falls are eased until they commence to render around the staghorn, and the boat to lower slowly.

When the coxswain, or officer in charge, sees that the boat is being towered, under control:

"Lower away" . . .	Boat is lowered more rapidly. Care must be exercised to keep it square and under control.

Should the boat become down by the bow or stern:

"Handsomely foremost fall"	Foremost fall is lowered more
or	slowly.
"Avast lowering after fall".	The after fall ceases to lower.

When the boat is square again:

"Lower away" . . .	Both falls are lowered together.

When the boat is in the water:

"Light to"	The hands lowering the boat let go the falls, and, taking them off the staghorn, overhaul sufficiently to enable the hands in the boat to unhook. The after fall is unhooked first. The falls are then rounded up; the lower blocks are secured to a slip at the foot of the davit; the falls are hauled taut and coiled down. The boat is pulled out to the boom, where the remainder of the crew man it.

HOISTING A BOAT

Order	*Action*
"Fxlemen reeve *1st cutter's* falls."	The falls are cast off from the slip at the foot of the davit and overhauled until the lower blocks are just clear of the

water low enough to hook on in the boat. The hauling parts are rove through the necessary leading blocks and led along the deck.

Note. The falls are usually rove by the part of the ship in which the davits are situated.

"Away, *1st cutter's* crew. Hook your boat on."

The boat is manned at the boom, and pulled under the davits. Bow and stroke oarsmen clear away the slings and hook on. The foremost fall being hooked on first, then take up their positions in the boat as for lowering. The remainder of the crew clear the boat.

While the boat is being hooked on, the necessary hands required for hoisting are piped to man the falls.

"*Port watch* up *1st cutter*"

The watch, or whatever party of hands is piped, man the falls of the boat referred to.

When the boat is hooked on, and the falls are manned, the coxswain reports, "All ready in the boat, sir," and the boatswain's mate reports "Falls manned, sir."

"Haul taut singly" . . . The falls are hauled taut separately, all hands keeping outside them and evenly distributed on either side.

"Marry" . . . . The falls are married,—*i.e.*, the two lines of men close together and grip both falls as one.

"Hoist away" . . . . The hands on the falls haul away and *run* the boat up.

When a boat is being run up the order "Walk" should be given before it is close up to the davit head:

"Walk"

The hands on the falls break into a walk and hoist the boat handsomely.

When the boat is close up to the davit head, and the falls are nearly two blocks:

"High enough" . . .	Hands on the falls cease hoisting and remain fast on the falls.

If the boat is not squarely horizontal between the davits:

"Separate the falls" . .	The falls are separated and opened out, the hands remaining on the falls their own side and facing towards the boat.
"After fall (or foremost fall) hoist"	This order is passed by the boatswain's mate as "Shipside fall" or "Midship fall." The fall named is hoisted until the order "High enough" is given.

When the boat is up, the bow and stroke oarsmen pass the life lines under the hook of the slings, up over the davit head, under the slings, and dog the end round all parts and back up. They report to the coxswain "All fast forward (or aft)," and he, when both are ready, reports "All fast in the boat, sir."

"Ease to the life lines" . .	Keeping the falls in hand, the hands manning them walk back towards the davits until the life lines take the weight of the boat.
"Light to" . . .	About two fathoms of the fall are hauled towards the davits, and the falls let go. The hands attending at the davits pass the fall over the fairlead on the davit, haul taut and belay the falls around the staghorn. The lifelines are then eased and the weight taken on the
"Unreeve boat's falls" . .	falls. The falls are then unrove and flaked down for running, or reeled up.

After a boat has been hoisted it must be squared off, both inside and outside. The outside will require to be wiped over, especially along the waterline. All oars, masts and sails must be stowed neatly, and the boat left level. The plug, which should be taken out as soon as the boat is clear of the water, should be left out except in a sea boat, of course.

In belaying a boat's fall, care must be taken to pass the first turn correctly, as this turn will be required for lowering on the next occasion of the boat being required. For all sea boats a special staghorn is fitted.

EXPRESSIONS AND ORDERS USED WHEN HANDLING PULLING BOATS

The following expressions and orders are arranged in no particular sequence, and each must be viewed in conjunction with all the others.

It should be noted that in every case where an order is given to the crew or any member of it while they are pulling, the order should be given when the blades are in the water and one more stroke should be given before the order is carried out.

"Oars!"	The position of 'attention' in a pulling boat. The oars are held at right angles to the boat, parallel to the surface of the water, the blades horizontal. Bodies should be upright and arms slightly bent.
"Shove off!"	The boat is shoved away from the ship or jetty, usually bows first, the bowman using the wooden end of his boathook.
"Give way together!" . .	The crew, taking their time from the stroke oar, commence pulling.
"Way enough!" . . .	This is the order to stop pulling. In double-banked boats, other than those being used as sea boats, the oars are 'tossed.' In single-banked boats, other than sea boats, the crew lie back, allowing the loom of the oar to pass over then-heads, and the blade to go aft. (see expression "Boat oars.")

"Toss your oars!" . . .	Only done in a double-banked boat. The oars are brought to a vertical position, blades fore and aft.
"Oars down!" . . .	This is the executive order for coming to the position of 'oars.' If necessary it can be used for port or starboard oars only.
"Ship your oars!" . . . *or* "Oars ready!"	The oars are placed in the crutches' in a single-banked boat, or the 'rowlocks' in a double banked boat.
"Boat your oars!" . .	In a double-banked boat the oars are laid fore and aft in the boat with the *blades for-word,* and outboard of the crew.
	In a single-banked boat the oars are lifted out of the crutches, and laid fore and aft in the boat, blades aft and outboard of the crew (see "Bows"; in a single-banked boat the only oar laid with the blade forward is the bowman's).
"Bows!" . . .	This is an order given prepa-ratory to coming alongside, for the bowman to lay in his oar, and man his boathook. In a double-banked boat the bow-men toss their oars together, touch the blades (termed 'Kissing'), and boat them by sliding the looms aft, amid-ships in the boat. In a single-banked boat, the bowman lifts his oar out of the crutch and boats it by sliding the loom aft.
"Hold water!"	This order is given when it is desired to take all way off the boat. The blades of the oars

	are held firmly in the water, at right angles to the boat.
"Back together!" "Back starboard!" "Back port!"	This order is given when it is desired to move the boat astern, or turn her short round. The oars referred to are given the opposite motion through the water to when 'giving way.'
Feather	The oars are said to be feathered when the blades are fore and aft.
"Fenders in!" *or* "Fenders out!"	Each member of the crew is responsible that there is nothing hanging over the side of the boat in his immediate vicinity. When coming alongside fenders are put out on the side that is liable to rub. On leaving the ship or jetty they are immediately brought inboard.

CREWS OF POWER BOATS

The number in the crew of a power boat depends, naturally, on the size of the power boat. A small power boat's crew will probably consist of a **coxswain**, a **bowman**, a **stern sheetman**, and a stoker.

In big power boats there may be two bowmen and two stern sheetmen.

The Coxswain. The coxswain is in complete charge of his boat when away from the ship and when there is no executive officer present.

The Bowman. The bowman is responsible for the securing and fending of the forward end of the boat when alongside, and for bearing off when leaving a ship's side or jetty. He uses a boat hook.

He is also responsible that there is nothing hanging over the side in the fore part of the boat, when under way or at the boom.

His cleaning duties in the boat will be detailed by the coxswain.

The Stern Sheetman. His duties are the same as the bowman's except that he is concerned with the after end of the boat. When his other duties allow he should also assist passengers in and out of the boat.

The Stoker. In large power boats there may be a stoker P.O. He is entirely responsible for the engines of the boat. He must obey all orders that come to him from the coxswain by bell, voice pipe or telegraph.

CHAPTER VII

MISCELLANEOUS

ORGANISATION OF A SHIP

The primary consideration for the organisation of any of H.M. ships is, and always has been, her fighting efficiency.

The secondary consideration is naturally her working efficiency, and it will be seen that these two go hand in hand.

Fighting Efficiency

In time of war the most efficient method of keeping the ship in a constant state of readiness to engage the enemy is to have the men 'closed up' at their fighting positions or 'action stations' the whole of the time that the ship is at sea, but if the ship is at sea a long time in the hope of meeting the enemy, it is obvious that individual efficiency will be impaired by the tiredness of the men.

Therefore a watch system is required.

Working Efficiency

The routine work of a ship still carries on even in wartime, and a watch system is necessary both in harbour and at sea.

At **sea**, because one watch is closed up at their 'cruising stations,' while the other watch does the work necessary and rests.

In **harbour**, because one watch is on shore leave and the other on board to do the necessary work, and, in the event of a ship receiving 'immediate' sailing orders, to take the ship to sea and be capable of fighting her.

WATCH ORGANISATION

Having seen the reasons for a watch organisation, the systems in use in the Royal Navy will now be considered.

(1) Two Watches

The ship's company is divided into two halves called the port and **starboard** watches.

Each watch is again divided up into two halves, called the 1st and 2nd **parts** of the watch.

In ships which have a large complement, generally speaking

cruisers and above, the parts of watch are still further subdivided into two parts called the **sub** (subdivision) of watch.

Thus the situation now is as follows:

Port watch $\begin{cases} \text{1st part} \begin{cases} \text{1st sub.} \\ \text{2nd sub.} \end{cases} \\ \text{2nd part} \begin{cases} \text{3rd sub.} \\ \text{4th sub.} \end{cases} \end{cases}$ **Starboard** $\begin{cases} \text{1st part} \begin{cases} \text{1st sub.} \\ \text{2nd sub.} \end{cases} \\ \text{2nd part} \begin{cases} \text{3rd sub.} \\ \text{4th sub.} \end{cases} \end{cases}$

(2) Three Watches

These consist of **red, white,** and **blue** watches, and are only used in ships with a large complement, where not more than one-third of the ship's company is closed up at **'cruising'** stations and the other two-thirds are employed in their part of ship, or resting. Generally this is only used when the ship is at sea.

The engine-room personnel nearly always use the three-watch system, both at sea and in harbour.

DIVISIONAL ORGANISATION

As an additional means of obtaining working efficiency the ship is divided up into **parts of ship,** the number depending on the size of the ship (see sketches below), and an officer, generally of lieutenant's rank,

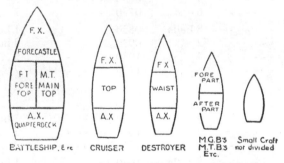

Fig. 66

is placed in charge of each. He is referred to as the **divisional officer**, and is responsible for the general welfare, requests and discipline of the men in his division. The ship's company is divided equally between each **part of ship**, so that there are equal numbers of higher ratings (*i.e.,* C.P.O.s, P.O.s, L.Sea., etc.) and equal numbers of gunnery rates in each part of ship.

The men in each part of ship are divided equally among the watches.

TIME

In the Royal Navy the day is divided into seven parts, called watches which are named as follows (*Note:* The 24.00 hours' system is used):

0000 to 0400 (midnight to 4 A.M.)	. .	**Middle watch**
0400 to 0800 (4 A.M. to 8 A.M.)	. .	**Morning watch**
0800 to 1200 (8 A.M. to noon)	. .	**Forenoon watch**
1200 to 1600 (Noon to 4 P.M.)	. .	**Afternoon watch**
1600 to 1800 (4 P.M. to 6 P.M.)	. .	**First dog watch**
1800 to 2000 (6 P.M. to 8 P.M.)	. .	**Last dog watch**
2000 to 0000 (8 P.M. to midnight)	. .	**First watch**

On board ship time is marked every half-hour by striking a bell, the number of strokes giving the time, as follows:

Midnight

0000	- - - - - - - -	8 bells	0030	-	1 bell
0100	- -	2 ,,	0130	- - -	3 bells
0200	- - - -	4 ,,	0230	- - - - -	5 ,,
0300	- - - - - -	6 ,,	0300	- - - - - - -	7 ,,
0400	- - - - - - - -	8 bells	0430	-	1 bell
0500	- -	2 ,,	0530	- - -	3 bells
0600	- - - -	4 ,,	0630	- - - - -	5 ,,
0700	- - - - - -	6 ,,	0730	- - - - - - -	7 ,,
0800	- - - - - - - -	8 bells	0830	-	1 bell
0900	- -	2 ,,	0930	- - -	3 bells
1000	- - - -	4 ,,	1030	- - - - -	5 ,,
1100	- - - - - -	6 ,,	1130	- - - - - - -	7 ,,

Noon

1200	- - - - - - - -	8 bells	1230	-	1 bell
1300	- -	2 ,,	1330	- - -	3 bells
1400	- - - -	4 ,,	1430	- - - - -	5 ,,
1500	- - - - - -	6 ,,	1530	- - - - - - -	7 ,,
1600	- - - - - - - -	8 bells	1630	-	1 bell
1700	- -	2 ,,	1730	- - -	3 bells
1800	- - - -	4 bells	1830	-	1 bell
1900	- -	2 ,,	1930	- - -	3 bells
2000	- - - - - - - -	8 bells	2030	-	1 bell
2100	- -	2 ,,	2130	- - -	3 bells
2200	- - - -	4 ,,	2230	- - - - -	5 ,,
2300	- - - - - -	6 ,,	2330	- - - - - - -	7 ,,

REQUESTS AND COMPLAINTS

On the notice board of every ship and shore establishment there is posted a copy of the regulations concerning this matter. It is a copy of the Articles of the King's Regulations and Admiralty Instructions on the subject, and each man should make a point of reading it.

The divisional officer lays down in his orders the time that routine requests are to be handed in to the divisional petty officer, and also the time that request men will be interviewed.

Requests or complaints must go through the 'proper service channels,' as follows:

Requests

The request must be made out in the following form:

'Request to see the Captain through the Commander, through the Divisional Officer, to be rated Able Seaman.'

The request is given to the divisional officer through the divisional petty officer.

If any man wishes to prefer a request which requires immediate action (*e.g.*, compassionate leave on receipt of a telegram informing the man that his next-of-kin is dying) he must carry out the same routine—*i.e.*, hand his request to the divisional or duty petty officer, who will take him at once before the appropriate authority. This can be done at any time of day or night.

If any man wishes to consult his captain or divisional officer on a very private or domestic matter, he must carry out the same routine.

The officer concerned will ensure privacy by sending everyone away out of ear-shot. However, there is only one point to remember, the request must be of a private or domestic nature, which has nothing to do with service matters.

Complaints

If any man has any cause for complaint of injustice or ill-treatment, there is a service method of obtaining redress. Any other method is strictly forbidden.

The method is to request through the aforementioned service channels 'to state a complaint.'

There are four rules to be observed:

(1) The complaint must be confined to a statement of facts.
(2) Joint complaints (*i.e.*, 'round Robins') are strictly forbidden. Each man must make his own complaint.

(3) It is an offence to make a complaint stating any untrue facts to the knowledge of complainant.

(4) Disrespectful or insubordinate language is an offence, except where such language is necessary when explaining the complaint.

N.B. It is **not** an offence to state a complaint. No Petty Officer or man shall be penalized for having made a complaint in accordance with these rules.

Every order must be obeyed. A rating who receives an order which he considers unjust must obey first and make his complaint afterwards.

TOBACCO REGULATIONS

The issue of duty-free tobacco to the **Royal Navy** is a privilege which is not afforded to any other force of the Crown, therefore this privilege must be most jealously guarded. It may be a temptation to take more tobacco or cigarettes ashore than the regulations prescribe. Remember, therefore, not only is it a grave offence to smuggle, or attempt to do so; but the offender might be the cause of having this privilege stopped for the whole of the Royal Navy.

Monthly Issue. Officers and men are allowed to 'take up' one pound of tobacco each month on the home station and two pounds on a foreign station. It is an offence for anyone to 'take up' his tobacco and sell or give it away.

Landing Tobacco. Men are allowed to take one ounce or 20 cigarettes ashore each night up to **six** nights.

For seven or more nights the maximum amount that can be landed is one-half of a pound or 160 cigarettes.

If more is required to be landed by any man he has to pay duty on the excess, onboard, to a Customs official and obtain a landing pass for it.

Proceeding to Hospital. Not more than 1 pound of tobacco may be landed on proceeding to hospital. The amount must be declared on the sick note accompanying the patient.

Transfer by Land. One pound of service or gift tobacco, and either 2 ounces of tobacco or 50 cigarettes of a gift or proprietary brand (in Home waters), can be taken with a man when transferred by land from one ship or establishment to another.

In foreign waters the amount is 2 pounds of service tobacco.

Parcel Post. Dutiable goods must not be posted from any of H.M. ships unless the full duty has been paid on them and a receipt obtained from the Customs officials.

SLINGING A HAMMOCK

Hammock: The canvas part, having 16 holes in each end, usually fitted with eyelets.

Clews. 'A set of clews' consists of two **lanyards**, each spliced to its metal ring, each ring carrying eight **nettles** (six-foot lengths of 3-stranded white hemp ⅝ inch in circumference), for slinging the two ends of the hammock.

The nettles are first middled, with the eye so formed secured with a racking seizing; the eye is passed through the ring and secured by passing the two ends through the eye. As each nettle has two ends, sixteen ends are thus provided, one for each eyelet hole in the end of the hammock.

Lashing. A length of sisal long enough to allow the **seven** turns to be taken round the hammock and secured to its own part. The lashing has an eye-splice at one end and may be 'pointed' at the other.

To sling the hammock secure one lanyard to the hammock bar overhead so that the ends of the nettles hang at the level of the chest. Pass the outer nettles through the outer corner eyelet holes at one end of the hammock and secure by a half-hitch, leaving about six inches of the ends hanging down. Then take the two nettles nearest the centre and secure them to their corresponding eyelet holes in the centre of the hammock-end, leaving about **four** inches hanging down. Then secure the remaining nettles in like manner from the centre outwards, leaving increasing lengths of end hanging.

Repeat with the other end of the hammock and the other clews. Plait the ends of the nettles up in threes, leaving them inside the hammock.

Sling the hammock between two hammock bars by passing the lanyard over the bar, back up through its own ring and form a sheet bend over the nettles. Then distribute the bedding evenly over the length of the hammock and tauten up the slack nettles if necessary.

To keep the head of the hammock apart a stretcher can be used, but this is optional. It consists of a length of wood about two feet in length with a V cut out at both ends. These V's take over the top two nettles on each side.

To Lash up a Hammock

Distribute the bedding evenly over the length of the hammock leaving about six inches clear at each end to prevent bunches of bedding and blankets oozing out of the ends when it is lashed.

Lower the hammock until it is breast high, and stand on the left side facing the head. Pass the lashing over the hammock and reeve

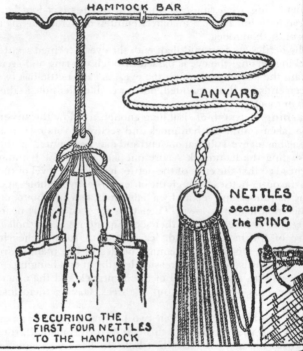

SECURING THE CLEWS OF A HAMMOCK

HAMMOCK BAR

LANYARD

NETTLES
secured to
the RING

SECURING THE
FIRST FOUR NETTLES
TO THE HAMMOCK

LASHING

THE FIRST TURN IS PASSED THRO' THE EYE OF THE LASHING.
THE NEXT FIVE TURNS ARE MARLINE-HITCHED.
THE LAST TURN IS HALF-HITCHED TO ITS OWN PART

Fig. 67

the end through the eye and draw taut; this is the first turn. The succeeding turns are taken as follows:—

Coil the lashing up and pass it up and over the hammock with the right hand and bring it under the hammock into the left hand then over its own standing part and haul taut by swinging back on it. This hitch is called a marline hitch.

The final turn is taken around the neck of the hammock at the foot and is secured on its own part by a half-hitch. The end is then passed neatly along the hammock under each turn.

The clews are stowed by twisting the nettles round right-handed and tucking under the turns of lashing along the hammock.

HINTS ON KIT

(1) Always keep clothes brushed and stowed away neatly when not in use and always remember that there is a method of stowing clothes in a **kit-bag** (*vide* Seamanship Manual, vol. I) which prevents bad creasing.

(2) Always stow white clothing apart from the blue, and if any bad stains (*e.g.*, black oil) appear on the clothes, a little soap rubbed on the spot will make it easier to remove. If possible, wrap up whites to prevent them picking up green or brown stain from the kit bag.

(3) **Boots**. These must not be crosslaced. Laceends and boot tags must be tucked away neatly.

(4) **Trousers.** The botttoms must just touch the instep of the foot. The flaps must always be buttoned up.

(5) **Jerseys and Flannels.** The top must be kept in a straight line across the neck, not hanging in a V.

(6) **Jumpers.** These must always be pulled down to the full extent. Bulky things must not be stowed in the pocket: they cause an unsightly bulge, and are apt to fall out.

(7) **Silk.** The ends are sewn together. The bight is tied by the tapes, and must not be tucked inside the V of the jumper.

(8) **Tapes.** The object of the tapes is to hold the bight of the silk at the bottom of the V of the jumper. They must be seven inches long and tied round a two-inch long bight of the silk in a reef bow.

(9) **Collars.** The securing tapes must always be firmly tied round the body. When washed, the blue dye of the collar is apt to run into the white tapes if first put into hot water. To help prevent this it is a good thing to soak the collar in cold water before washing.

(10) **Cap.** This must always be worn square on the head. Chin-stays must be sewn into the requisite length for comfortable me. The cap must never be used as an additional pocket.

(11) **Cap Ribbon**. The cap ribbon must be worn so that the 'H.M.S.' is directly over the nose. **It must be tied in a reef bow over the left ear.**

(12) **Lanyard**. The knot of the lanyard must be three inches above the tapes. The bight of the lanyard under the silk must not hang down too low.

(13) **Overcoats and Scarves**. When wearing an overcoat its collar must never be turned up except in very bad weather, and then it must be buttoned up in front.

Scarves must be worn only for their proper purpose and not as a decoration, such as hanging down in front underneath the silk.

(14) **Kit Inspection**. A kit is to be laid out for inspection as shown in the diagram on opposite page.

The sketch shows the minimum kit of a Hostilities Only rating, who is **wearing** a serge suit, a collar and silk, a jersey, a pair of boots, a blue cap, a flannel and pair of drawers.

The regulation active service seaman's compulsory kit is shown below. (Separate instructions have been issued regarding the kits of Patrol Service ratings (R.N. and R.N.R.), of men entered specially for service in Boom Defence Vessels or for local defence duties and of apprentices and boys in Training Establishments.)

2 jumpers, serge.	1 jersey.
2 pairs trousers, serge.	1 knife.
2 jumpers, duck.	1 knife lanyard.
2 pairs trousers, duck.	1 soap bag.
1 overall suit.	1 comb.
2 collars, blue jean.	1 hair brush.
2 caps, blue or white.	1 tooth brush.
1 cap box.	1 clothes brush.
2 cap ribbons.	2 boot brushes.
1 scarf, black silk.	1 type.
2 pairs socks or stockings.	1 attaché case.
2 pairs boots or 1 pair boots and	2 pairs drawers.
1 pair shoes.	2 towels.
1 bed.	1 waistbelt.
1 blanket.	1 oilskin coat.
2 bed covers.	Vol. I, Seamanship Manual or
2 cotton 'flannels.'	Seaman's Pocket-book.
2 singlets.	

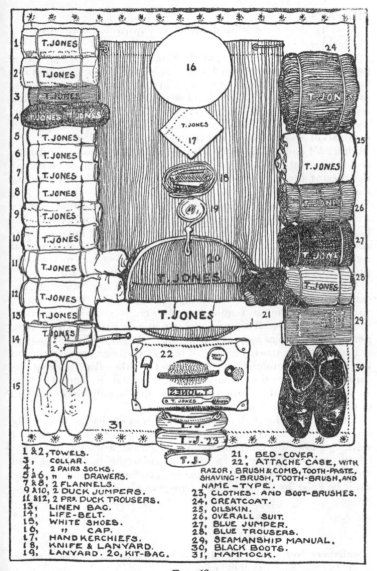

1 & 2, TOWELS.	21, BED-COVER.
3, COLLAR.	22, ATTACHE CASE, WITH
4, 2 PAIRS SOCKS.	RAZOR, BRUSH & COMB, TOOTH-PASTE,
5 & 6, " " DRAWERS.	SHAVING-BRUSH, TOOTH-BRUSH, AND
7 & 8, 2 FLANNELS.	NAME-TYPE.
9 & 10, 2 DUCK JUMPERS.	23, CLOTHES- AND BOOT-BRUSHES.
11 & 12, 2 PRS. DUCK TROUSERS.	24, GREATCOAT.
13, LINEN BAG.	25, OILSKIN.
14, LIFE-BELT.	26, OVERALL SUIT.
15, WHITE SHOES.	27, BLUE JUMPER.
16, " CAP.	28, BLUE TROUSERS.
17, HANDKERCHIEFS.	29, SEAMANSHIP MANUAL.
18, KNIFE & LANYARD.	30, BLACK BOOTS.
19, LANYARD. 20, KIT-BAG.	31, HAMMOCK.

FIG. 68

SIGNALS

Plate II shows the **alphabetical** and **numeral flags** used by H.M. ships.*

Plate III shows some **special flags**. Plate IV shows **naval pendants**. Sometimes a signal requires the same flag or pendant to be hoisted in several places at once, and to avoid the necessity for carrying extra sets of flags and lockers, etc., **substitutes** are employed for repeating a particular flag or pendant. Substitutes repeat the first, second, third and fourth flags of a series, and the first and second pendants of a series. These substitutes are shown in Plate V.

Plates VI and VII give the **Morse code**, the phonetic alphabet, and the special Morse signs for punctuation, etc. They also show sketches of the four types of lamp usually employed in flashing signals.

Plate VIII shows the **semaphore** signs and significations as they would appear to the reader of the message. On the signal-tower, Flag E is hoisted singly, indicating that a general semaphore signal is about to be sent. The semaphore arms are displaying the alphabetical sign '**J**,' and a rating is standing on top of the tower making the same sign with hand flags to ships lying beyond it on the far side.

When a semaphore message is addressed to one ship only the distinguishing pendants of that ship are hoisted superior to flag E, and only that ship is required to answer. A general semaphore message addresses all ships, and each ship hoists her **answering pendant** close up as soon as she is ready to begin reading the signal.

Flag hoists are usually answered by the Answering pendant when that signal is understood. If, however, the flags cannot be distinguished, or the meaning of the signal is doubtful, the Answering pendant is hoisted 'at the dip,' that is, only three-quarters of the way up to the yard, instead of 'close up.'

Although visual signalling in the Navy is in the hands of specially trained men of the Communications Branch, every seaman needs a working knowledge of the meaning of flags and pendants, and of the morse and semaphore codes. In particular, he must be able to recognise his own ship's distinguishing pendants, whether these are made by hoist, by flashing, or by semaphore.

---

*Publishers' Note: Plates II, III, IV & V are reproduced in colour on the front and back endpapers of this edition.

MORSE CODE & PHONETIC ALPHABET

A	ABLE
B	BAKER
C	CHARLIE
D	DOG
E	EASY
F	FOX
G	GEORGE
H	HOW
I	ITEM
J	JIG
K	KING
L	LOVE
M	MIKE
N	NAN
O	OBOE
P	PETER
Q	QUEEN
R	ROGER
S	SUGAR
T	TARE
U	UNCLE
V	VICTOR
W	WILLIAM
X	X-RAY
Y	YOKE
Z	ZEBRA

10 INCH "S.P."

1
2
3
4
5
6
7
8
9
0

BOX LAMP

PLATE VI

SPECIAL MORSE SIGNS

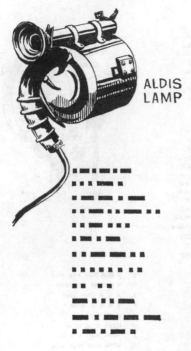

ALDIS LAMP

▬▬▬▬▬▬	FULL-STOP
▪ ▪ ▪	GENERAL CALL
▬▬ ▪ ▬▬	PENDANT SIGN
▪ ▬▬ ▪ ▪ ▬▬ ▪	FLAG SIGN
▬▬ ▪ ▬▬	NUMERAL SIGN
▪ ▬▬ ▪	LINK SIGN
▬▬ ▪ ▬▬ ▬▬	REPEAT
▪ ▪ ▪ ▪ ▪ ▪ ▪ ▪	ERASE
▪ ▪ ▪	SHORT BREAK SIGN
▬▬ ▪ ▪ ▪ ▬▬	LONG BREAK SIGN
▬▬ ▪ ▬▬ ▪ ▬▬	NEGATIVE
▪ ▬▬ ▪ ▬▬ ▪	ENDING SIGN

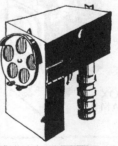

PATT. 1038 LAMP

PLATE VII

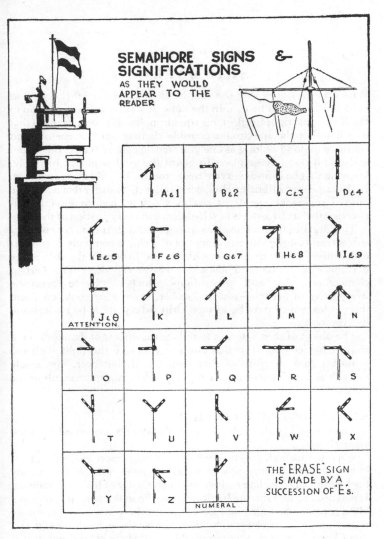

PLATE VIII

CHAPTER VIII
SHIP SAFETY

WHEN a boxer goes into the ring he aims to hit the other fellow as hard and as often as he can. In the same way every officer and man in the Navy must fight his fleet, his squadron, his ship, or his gun so that it will inflict the maximum possible damage on the enemy, and continue to do so as long as one gun remains above water. But a cool and skilful boxer remembers to guard the vital points of his body, knowing that he cannot survive many rounds by wild slogging alone. In the same way a fighting ship, which expects to suffer damage in the normal course of events at sea in wartime, has an organisation covering the broad aspects of self-defence in every portion of the ship.

This organisation is known as damage control. It is a very complex subject, and all the various branches of a ship's company have their own duties in operating the machinery and fittings in the ship in the best way to withstand damage. However, there are certain elementary rules and precautions which apply to everyone irrespective of branch—seaman, stoker, marine, or cook, etc., and these rules, which may be termed **ship safety**, must be understood by everyone.

The object of ship safety is to reduce the effects of damage on the ship or her company so that she can continue the fight with the utmost vigour in spite of that damage. If, however, one single individual fails in carrying out the ship safety rules, the result of the ship's ability to fight may be disastrous.

KNOWLEDGE OF YOUR SHIP

The first and golden rule where ship's safety is concerned is, **know your ship.**

We often marvel, when watching a blind person move about his house, at the unerring way in which he progresses, but it is only because he has complete and accurate knowledge of his surroundings. It may well be that during battle you may be in the same position as a blind person—the lights may have failed or there may be dense smoke from fires and you can see nothing. Under those conditions, if you don't know your way about your ship and where everything in it is placed, you will be helpless.

During battle you may be entrusted with an important message but fail to deliver it because you cannot find your way through damaged and dark compartments. This lack of knowledge of your ship may have fatal consequences to your ship, your shipmates and yourself.

Take every opportunity, therefore, of finding out all you possibly can about the lay-out, routes and fittings in your ship. Don't confine your journeys to those required by your daily job; deliberately try and find other compartments, and never be afraid to ask the way.

DAMAGE

The damage which a ship can receive is very varied and complex, but everyone should know something about the main types, which are as follows:

(1) Flooding.
(2) Fire.
(3) Damage to machinery and equipment.
(4) Damage to personnel.

We will take each of these headings and discuss briefly the principal methods of competing with them, but it must be remembered that very often none of the rules laid down exactly applies to the situation, and the men on the spot must use their common sense and ability to improvise.

FLOODING

List. Flooding almost always results in the ship listing, but ships are constructed to be able to accept a large degree of list when damaged without capsizing.

To the uninitiated a small degree of list tends to be alarming—especially to those who cannot see what is going on in the outside world.

Don't become alarmed when list occurs—the ship is not going to sink because she is not upright.

The ship will fill up and sink as the result of flooding from damage unless steps are taken to stop or control the inflow of water. The following are the methods of achieving this:

(1) To confine the flooding to as small a part of the ship as possible. This is done by dividing the ship up into watertight compartments known as **watertight subdivision.**
(2) Stop the inflow through the hole.
(3) Pump out the water that has got into the ship or, if it is still flooding, keep it under control by pumping.

Compartments normally above the waterline must not be ignored as they are liable to be flooded after damage due to the lowering of the ship in the water.

We will now mention briefly the methods of dealing with flooding.

WATERTIGHT SUBDIVISION

The ship is divided up into a number of separate watertight compartments by bulkheads and decks, so as to reduce the extent of the flooding resulting from a hole below the waterline. But bulkheads and decks must be pierced by doors and hatches to allow access, and by pipelines and ventilation trunks.

The doors and hatches when shut are watertight, and where a pipe or trunk passes through a bulkhead or deck there is a valve on it, which is also watertight when shut.

Obviously the ship is in the best state to resist the spread of flooding after damage when all these fittings are closed, but that could not be accepted all the time, as men must move about the ship, and they must have air to breathe. It follows, therefore, that during the life of a ship some of these watertight fittings must be repeatedly opened and closed, and, to ensure that they are closed when they should be control markings are put on them to show when it is permissible for them to be open.

There are various markings, but they are simple and every man in the ship must know their meaning so that he can check that every watertight fitting is in the correct state for the condition of the ship at the moment, *i.e.*, harbour, cruising at sea, or in battle.

The scheme, applicable to all ships with watertight compartments, is shown in the table below, a copy of which should be posted up on the notice-board in your ship. It is essential that you should learn all you can about the closing of watertight doors, hatches, and valves in your ship and practise closing them. Failure to close even the smallest (*e.g.*, bathroom drain valves) may cause flooding to spread, with disastrous results.

The risk involved in leaving open a door, hatch or valves is shown in colour—**red** and **blue**.

IN EMERGENCY

Doors, hatches, and valves with **red** and **blue** markings
must be closed.

First close the **Red**, then close the **Blue**.

(Pipe 'Close **red** and **blue** openings' means that there is
an emergency.)

WATERTIGHT DISCIPLINE

The control of any particular opening is indicated by a lettered symbol:

X = Permission required to open.

Y = Can be opened for passage or use but must be reclosed at once. Permission required to keep open.

Z = When closed the "Y" rule applies.

O = Closed only when ordered.

Routine. Rules posted alongside. Read them.

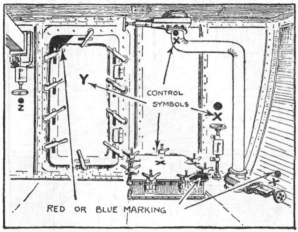

FIG. 69. TYPICAL COMPARTMENT SHOWING WATERTIGHT CONTROL MARKINGS.

In addition, there are qualifying symbols for special conditions such as 'Action,' 'Gas,' etc., but, as they do not alter the basic rules above, we will omit them here, though they must be studied and understood when you get to your ship.

If you are on a job which involves opening doors and hatches to let you pass through, such as getting up stores from below, it is your own personal duty to ensure that you **shut** and **clip** the doors when you have passed through. This applies in peace and in war, at sea or in harbour, and there is no excuse whatever for failure.

There have been many instances where negligence in this vital duty of properly closing doors, hatches, and valves has caused flooding to spread to undamaged compartments.

OBSTRUCTIONS TO TRAFFIC

Besides doors and hatches which have to be opened and closed, there are other fittings which impede traffic and which make it difficult to move about the ship. Sills and coamings, some 2 feet 6 inches high, and

FIG. 70. SPREAD OF FLOODING THROUGH OPEN VENTILATION VALVES.

dwarf bulkheads, are fitted extensively to reduce the area over which flood water will spread after damage.

Treat them as aids to preserving your ship and yourself, which they are, and not just as obstacles which hamper your movements.

VENTILATION SYSTEM

To get air to compartments low down in the ship, trunks are led from the upper deck to the spaces concerned.

Where trunks pass through decks and bulkheads shut off valves are fitted to safeguard watertightness. These valves are marked and controlled in a similar fashion to doors and hatches—X, Y, Z, etc.

If these valves are not closed the danger is that flooding will spread through the trunking to intact compartments. Once again, then, it is every man's duty to know what these symbols mean and to ensure that all ventilation valves are in the correct state according to their marking.

STOPPING THE INFLOW OF WATER

Unless the hole is fairly small, stopping the inflow will be difficult. With a small hole you may be able to control the inflow by plugging it up with shot plugs. These are wooden plugs supplied in different sizes. Alternatively, leak stopping mats can be used. These are small canvas mats for folding up and jamming in the hole. Improvisation with any material that may be handy may make an excellent substitute, if the above means are not immediately available.

If the hole is not too far below the waterline the inflow can sometimes be stopped by bringing the hole above the waterline, by lightening the ship, or listing her.

In small craft the latter may be an easy and quick method.

USE OF PUMPS

In a case of underwater damage, pumps can have two main functions; either to pump water out of the ship after the inflow has been stopped, or to control flooding by pumping water out as fast as it comes in.

There are various types of pumps supplied, ranging from small hand pumps to the large high-capacity electrically driven pumps.

STOWAGE OF KIT

One of your principal duties regarding pumps is to ensure that no pump gets its suction clogged up by floating debris due to your carelessness.

Every man in the ship has a big responsibility in this respect by stowing all his personal property correctly and securely in the lockers provided. To illustrate this, here are some examples of what may result from carelessness on this very important point.

(1) The shock of an explosion is great, and will result in badly secured locker doors flying open and releasing all the kit in the locker on to the deck. If flooding occurs as well, this gear will float, and trousers, jumpers, socks, etc., will get round the end of the suction hose and prevent the water from being pumped out.

(2) The same thing will occur if gear like caps, towels and books is stowed overhead on the tops of pipes and fan trunks, instead of in the lockers. It may be convenient to have a book near your slinging billet, but it will be a menace to the safety of your ship if it is there when she is hit.

SUCTION HOSE

FIG. 71. CHOKING OF PUMP SUCTION BY PERSONAL GEAR.

FIRE

Fire is one of the most common and one of the most dangerous forms of damage which a ship sustains, because of the amount of inflammable material carried, such as petrol, oil, paint, explosives, cleaning gear, bedding, etc.

Above all else, it is a form of damage which, firstly, must be dealt with by the man on the spot.

Reporting and getting help are secondary.

A small fire dealt with at once is comparatively harmless, but if not dealt with immediately it will spread very rapidly, with, possibly, disastrous results to the ship and those in her. It is, therefore, of prime importance that each individual should learn all he can about fires, and the equipment for controlling them.

To produce fire three ingredients are needed:

(1) An inflammable substance.
(2) A supply of air (oxygen).
(3) A supply of heat.

The removal of any one of these ingredients from a fire will put it out. It is almost impossible to remove the inflammable substance, so fire-fighting methods are concentrated on depriving the fire either of oxygen or heat.

To achieve the former various substances, such as foam, steam and special gases, are provided which cover the flames and prevent the air from getting to it, thus starving it of oxygen and putting it out.

Another means of starving the fire of oxygen if it is between decks, is to shut all doors, hatches and ventilation, so preventing a further supply of oxygen, and the fire will burn out when it has used up the oxygen in the burning compartment.

To deprive the fire of heat, water sprays and jets are supplied which will cool the burning material and put out the fire.

TYPES OF FIRE AND EXTINGUISHERS USED

The following is a list of some of the more common types of fire and the equipment supplied to deal with them:

Oil fuel. Sand, water spray (Nuswift apparatus) or spray nozzles, steam-drenching foam. **Never** a solid jet of water.
Diesel oil. Sand, foam, large spray nozzles (not Nuswift).
Electrical. Pyrene, sand, water spray (**never** a solid jet or foam).
Petrol. Foam, Pyrene, methyl-bromide (**not water**).
Paintwork, woodwork, bedding, etc. Water, preferably spray.

All the above is concerned with fires which have started, but prevention is always better than cure, and it is obviously wise to concentrate on reducing the chance of fire rather than on attacking the fire when it has broken out.

Here again there is a personal responsibility for each man in the ship; carelessness and selfishness can gravely increase the fire risk in his ship. The following are examples:

(1) Not returning paint pots to the paint shop after use.
(2) Stowing tins of oil and petrol in odd corners for convenience.
(3) Hoarding up private stores of cleaning gear, rope, etc., in your particular part of ship.
(4) Hiding anything inflammable where it will be difficult to get at if it catches fire.
(5) Carrying surplus kit and private gear, books, etc., on board.
(6) Retaining empty boxes, cartons and packings on board instead of making every effort to get them landed.

Lastly, fire is always accompanied by dense smoke, so be prepared for it by knowing your ship so well that you can find your way in darkness, and by knowing how to use the *breathing apparatus provided*, so that you can remain in the smoke and fight the fires.

In this connection an anti-gas respirator is **not** a self-contained breathing apparatus and, therefore, is almost valueless as a protection in smoke.

Remember, in its initial stage, fire is a matter for immediate action by **the man on the spot.**

DAMAGE TO MACHINERY AND EQUIPMENT

Under this heading comes every type of damage which may be inflicted on a ship, but which is not an immediate threat to the ship's ability to float.

Flooding, fire, or damage above and below the waterline may put out of action a gun, the steering gear, electric mains, the main engines or auxiliary machinery, or any other major or minor part of the ship's equipment.

To combat this type of damage the ship's organisation for breakdowns is made as perfect as possible, first on paper and then by drills. It is impossible to visualise and allow for every eventuality, and, therefore, great reliance must be placed on every individual.

There is only one way of making sure that you do the right thing in a crisis, and that is: **know your ship, know your own job**, and learn as much about the other man's job as you can.

DAMAGE TO PERSONNEL

The fighting efficiency of a ship may be reduced by casualties to as great a degree as by material damage. It is therefore your duty to the service, as well as to yourself, not to become a casualty when care on your part might prevent it.

When shells, bombs and torpedoes explode there is a large, intensely hot, momentary flash. It persists long enough, though, to inflict ghastly burns on bare skin, but the flimsiest covering will provide sufficient protection during its very short duration. In battle it is not only asking for acute pain, but helping the enemy, to allow any part of your body except the nose, mouth and eyes to be exposed.

ANTI-FLASH GEAR

Special clothing, called 'anti-flash' gear, is provided to protect the head and neck, and also gloves to cover hands and wrist, and this must always be worn during battle. The rest of the body should be covered by ordinary clothing, which provides good protection. Overalls must be properly buttoned; otherwise blast may blow them open, and the body be burned by flash.

In hot climates there is a tendency for men to go about partially uncovered, wearing only singlets above the waist, or with overalls open and sleeves cut off.

In battle this thoughtless practice may prove fatal.

FIRST AID

During an action other men may get wounded, and their lives may depend on the immediate action taken by those in the vicinity, therefore **know your first aid**. It may be that one of the casualties is a key-man at your action station and if there is no one to step into the breach your particular station ceases to function. It is up to you to see that this does not happen; therefore, **know the other man's job.**

YOUR SHIP

(1) Treat your ship as a personal friend—after all, you have to live together.

(2) Regard any orders that are issued to preserve your ship as sacred trusts, and something to be very careful about fulfilling, *not* as 'just another order' to be got round if possible.

(3) Never imagine that you are not personally concerned in every thing which menaces the safety of your ship. It doesn't matter what your job is, you have the same duty to your ship in giving her a helping hand when she needs it.

(4) Your ship is helpless without your assistance, make quite certain that no ignorance, carelessness or selfishness on your part will let her down when she enters the supreme ordeals of battle.

(5) The care of your ship in an emergency demands seamanship of the highest order.

APPLICATION AT SEA

After a short period in your ship you should be able to answer detailed questions arising out of this chapter applicable to your own particular ship.

DO YOU KNOW —

(1) The exact meaning of the colours and lettered symbols on doors, hatches and valves ?

(2) The right way to clip doors and close hatches?

(3) How your action station and mess deck are ventilated and where the valves are?

(4) How to work the different fire-fighting appliances?

(5) How to use a breathing apparatus?

(6) Routes and alternative routes to important centres—*e.g.*,
   damage control headquarters,
   main switchboard room,
   steering gear compartment, etc.?

(7) The various means of stopping leaks and splinter holes?

(8) That badly stowed clothes and gear choke pump suctions?

(9) That your own protection is important to your ship as well as yourself?

(10) Immediate first aid methods?

(11) How to use a telephone and give and take a message?

Examine yourself with questions like these at regular intervals to prove that you are a fit member of the ship's company.

Note: The terms listed below will be found printed in heavy type on the pages indicated.

INDEX

Conway
An imprint of Bloomsbury Publishing Plc
50 Bedford Square
London WC1B 3DP

www.bloomsbury.com

First published in 1943 by
HM Stationery Office, London
First Conway edition 2006
First Bloomsbury edition 2015

Reprinted 2016

Volume © Bloomsbury 2015

No responsibility for loss caused to any
individual or organization acting on or
refraining from action as a result of the
material in this publication can be accepted
by Bloomsbury or the author.

British Library Cataloguing-in-Publication Dat
A catalogue record for this book is available
from the British Library.

Library of Congress Cataloguing-in-Publication
data has been applied for.

ISBN 978-1-8448-6037-1

Printed and bound in Great Britain by
CPI Group (UK) Ltd, Croydon CR0 4YY